THE
COTTON
INDUSTRY
IN LONGDENDALE AND GLOSSOPDALE

THE
COTTON
INDUSTRY
IN LONGDENDALE AND GLOSSOPDALE

TOM QUAYLE

TEMPUS

To my daughters, Wendy and Penny. My grandchildren: Emily, Mellisa and Louisa, and my great granddaughter, Allana. Also to my son-in-laws Stephen and Ian and my friends, Willy, Gareth and Linda, and to my wife Bhing for her generous help, support and patience.

First published 2006

Tempus Publishing Limited
The Mill, Brimscombe Port,
Stroud, Gloucestershire, GL5 2QG
www.tempus-publishing.com

© Tom Quayle, 2006

The right of Tom Quayle to be identified as the Author
of this work has been asserted in accordance with the
Copyrights, Designs and Patents Act 1988.

British Library Cataloguing in Publication Data.
A catalogue record for this book is available from the British Library.

ISBN 0 7524 3883 2

Typesetting and origination by Tempus Publishing Limited.
Printed in Great Britain.

CONTENTS

ACKNOWLEDGEMENTS

Sincere thanks to all the following people for their invaluable help in writing this book.

I was privileged to have access to much information on Longdendale and Glossopdale cotton mills and works. I thank my former employers, MCWW (now United Utilities), for their cooperation.

I am indebted to the Glossop Library staff for their cooperation in helping me to research information on the mills of Glossop and the history of the council members and dignitaries who served the borough, many of whom were mill-owners.

Much of the history of the Glossop mills was obtained from R. Hamnett's regular newspaper column from the *Glossop Recorder* newspaper (*Glossop Reporter*) deposited in the Glossop Library which were written and recorded by the great local historian and journalist of his day, Robert Hamnett (1855–1914).

I am also deeply indebted to Mike Brown and Sue Hickinson of Glossop Heritage for their in-depth knowledge of the history of Glossop's cotton mills, paper mills, works, etc., and also for supplying old photographs of many Glossop mills. Thanks also to Mike for helping to check the proofs.

Posthumous thanks to Willy Sharpe of Tintwistle who was employed by Manchester Corporation and was assigned by them to research the mills in the Longdendale and Glossop area when M.C.W.W. were preparing their Water Compensation Act of 1954. I was fortunate to learn and benefit from all his great local knowledge and history, which I recorded.

Many thanks also to the helpful staffs of:
Glossop Heritage Centre
Liverpool Maritime Museum
Liverpool Reference Library
Manchester Central Reference Library
Tameside Library

Finally to Tempus Publishing Ltd, for their faith in publishing my second book.

I

QUEEN COTTON RULED

Simple cotton plant. How unassuming you are. Yet you became a Queen. Without fuss, Mother Nature cleverly conceived you of distinctive cellular hair, attached to tiny cotton seeds. You rightfully laid claim to be amongst the most valuable of Mother Nature's productions, for didn't she create you to grow the raw material for one of the world's greatest industries producing pure cotton goods? Was it not you who gave us so much rich history of right and wrong? So much harsh injustice between the white and the black races. So much conflict between the mill-owner and the British mill-worker. So much inequality between the rich and the poor. Yet you clothed Kings. You clothed Nations. You even clothed beggars. No wonder simple cotton plant, with your fine cellular hair, you became Queen of the Cotton Industry. We bow to you – Cotton Queen of the North.

Known in Peru even before the Incas and known in China at the time of the earliest dynasties, cotton ranks amongst one of man's earliest finds. The most ancient cotton-growing country is probably India, growing famous Indian Cottons. India was the forerunner in the advancement of hand weaving and spinning and also in the development of cotton fabrics. India built a flourishing business in cotton goods with other countries, including Egypt, Greece, and the Roman Empire. In time India became the largest country in the world producing cotton, and even today remains dominant in the production of cotton fabrics, some of which have never been equalled.

When Christopher Columbus set out to discover the New World and arrived by chance in the West Indies in 1492, the natives who befriended him greeted him with gifts of cotton. To his amazement he learned later that they had spun the yarn on a distaff, simply a stick with a cleft end in which is held the flax from which thread is drawn in spinning, yet the yarn possessed a remarkable finesse in quality, without the advantages of any type of machinery.

The manufacture of linen was brought over from the Netherlands to Britain by Protestant refugees, around the close of the sixteenth or early seventeenth century. That this manufacture was carried on in England at an early period of the seventeenth century we know on good authority from Lewis Robert's book, *Treasures of Traffic*, published in the year 1641, in which he states:

> The town of Manchester buys linen yarn from the Irish in great quantity, and weaving it, returns the same again into Ireland to sell. Neither does her industry rest here; for they buy

New Orleans cotton plant. The bolls are the fruit of the plant and whilst it is growing, hold the fluffy white cotton fibre called lint, together with about thirty seeds.

cotton wool in London that comes from Cyprus and Smyrna (formally Izmir, city and port in west Turkey) and work the same into fustians (thick twilled cotton fabric), vermillions (vivid red fabric), and dimities (crisp cotton fabric with raised stripes or checks), which they return to London where they are sold, and from thence not seldom are sent into such foreign ports, where the first material may be more easily had for that manufacture.

The establishment of two of the great stable trades of the cotton and woollen manufactures in Lancashire and Derbyshire, is no doubt mainly due to many local peculiarities and advantages. The innumerable small streams of excellent water, fed by copious rain which falls on the hills and moors, and the many natural facilities for communicating with the great markets and seaports, all combined to foster that extraordinary commercial prosperity and that rapid growth of population which were the distinguishing features of old England.

These goods were woven chiefly around the Glossop area of Derbyshire and the Bolton area of Lancashire, and then sold at their weekly markets mainly to the Manchester merchants, who afterwards finished them, then either sent them to London for export, or sold them to their customers all over the country. At this period, and for a long time afterwards, the weaver provided his own warp, which was of linen yarn, and used cotton wool for his weft. As a vast amount of time was lost seeking out these materials, agents for their sale were established in the northern villages by the Manchester merchants. This encouraged more and more weavers' cottages to form their own separate and independent little cottage factories.

At this early period of manufacture, the amount of different thick-twilled cotton fabrics with a short nap (fustians) were so numerous that it was estimated that there were over 2,000 different kinds over Britain, Europe, and America. Yarn thickness is determined by the number of times the standard length of yarn is spun, and this is determined using the thickness number of a single strand of spun yarn; the amount of spinning and the number of plies (strands) produce the yarn count. It should be noted that the thickness of yarn produced in England by the one-thread wheel – the only spinning machine known at that time – was very limited compared with the later multi-spindle machines of the cotton mills.

An interesting comparison of the lifestyle of a weaver was given by Samuel Bamford (1788–1872), an English radical reformer of the eighteenth century, who described in detail a cotton weaver's cottage in Lancashire at that time:

It consisted of one principal room which he called 'the house' and on the same floor was a loom shop capable of containing four looms, and in the rear of 'the house' was a small kitchen and a buttery. Over the house and loom shop were chambers, and over the kitchen and buttery was another small apartment. The whole of the rooms were lighted by windows of small square panes, framed in lead, those in the front being protected by shutters. Inside were a dozen good rush-bottomed chairs, the backs and rails bright with wax and rubbing, a handsome clock in mahogany case, a good chest of oaken drawers, a mahogany snap-table, a mahogany corner cupboard, all were well polished, besides tables, a weather glass, cornice and ornaments.

With the coming of the Industrial Revolution, a weaver's life became so different from this rather cosy romantic picture of the cottage cotton trade.

II

THE INDUSTRIAL REVOLUTION

The history of the cotton mills is one of the most fascinating periods of the Industrial Revolution and one of the most exciting. Many proclaim that the Industrial Revolution is simply defined as 'The application of power-driven machinery in manufacturing', but it is far more complicated than that, and it did not happen overnight. It was the outcome of a movement begun centuries earlier, when the discoveries of new lands in the fifteenth and sixteenth centuries opened up the possibility of increased trade and commerce. In the eighteenth century, the Industrial Revolution began to manifest itself, so a decisive change from an agricultural economy to an industrial economy began around 1740, and this movement gathered pace until roughly between 1760 and 1830, when change was so rapid as to deserve the term 'revolutionary'. Merchandise that had traditionally been made first in the home and then in small workshops began to be manufactured in the factory, and this led to the growth of towns, as people moved from their rural areas in search of work. Eighteenth-century Britain was still far from being a country of capitalistic enterprise but it was the first step in modern economic growth and development; and Great Britain led the way.

In the various parts of Britain where the woollen industry had located itself, the capitalistic tendencies had been developed on a large scale, and by 1760 cotton was still only a small industry compared to wool, and at best the cotton industry was only in an intermediate stage of this progression. The great importance of wool is mirrored in the presence of the 'Woolsack' upon which the Lord Chancellor sits in Parliament. It was introduced by King Edward III (1327–1377), and was stuffed with English wool as a reminder of the wealth and prosperity England traditionally derived from the wool trade.

The iron and coal industries employed comparatively few people – other capitalistic enterprises were not so typical. The agricultural interest was still dominant, and the hand craftsmen were still more important than the industrial or commercial capitalists.

The power of wind had been used for centuries to drive corn-grinding mills, but some looked for a way of driving machinery by some force more effective than the human hand but less capricious than wind or animals. This was first solved by the use of water power. Although water was already used by corn and flour mill owners to drive their millstones and grind their meal, water began to take on a new and important significance. The principle of the mill-wheel driven by the millstream was applied to other machinery on a larger scale.

Waterwheel of a typical cotton mill of the early nineteenth century (1827). Transmission gearing originally believed to belong to the famous Richard Arkwright. Wheel in foreground is 21ft in diameter and 7ft wide, developing 30hp.

Horizontal and vertical-shaft wooden waterwheels had been working in Europe since Roman times, long before John Smeaton was born, providing power for a large number of industrial purposes. As the Industrial Revolution began, water power was rapidly gaining momentum. John Smeaton was born at Austhorpe Lodge, near Leeds, in 1724, where he died of a stroke in 1794. More than 100 years later, Smeaton was still being quoted as a leading authority on waterwheel design. He patented his first waterwheel after first experimenting using a 2ft-diameter model undershot waterwheel with flat paddles comprising a wooden supply tank, giving a maximum head of 3ft above the bed of the channel, a discharge sump in the base, and a pump for raising water to the tank. In 1769, he constructed his first waterwheel built of wood, but the rings segments were bolted together by iron plates and the gudgeons were of iron. John Smeaton was one of the greatest of the eighteenth-century pioneer civil/mechanical engineer waterwheel designers – he even designed waterwheels for gunpowder mills. As the demand for power grew, a more efficient type of wheel was sought. Six years before Smeaton published his findings in 1754, he scientifically experimented using two types of paddles on waterwheel models. He discovered that more power was generated using overshot paddles, which he found were twice as effective as his previously designed undershot paddles. And this was fifteen years before Watt had patented his first steam engine in 1769.

Water-rights were so important they counted as part of the assets of a cotton mill. If a mill changed hands, which they often did many times, water-rights could increase the value of the mill by several thousand pounds. In some places, the right to use water was shared out by the mill-owners, but in most places there would only be one user, who would jealously guard his rights.

Water was extracted from the river or stream by means of a weir or dam built across its width. This raised the water level sufficiently to allow the stream of water, called the 'head', to flow by gravity along the millrace or goit. The flowing water was controlled by a sluice valve or gate to direct it onto the waterwheel or to divert the water elsewhere for other uses. In times of flooding the efficiency of a waterwheel could often be reduced by debris obstructing the free movement of the wheel in the tailrace, where the spent water normally escaped back into the river or stream.

Waterwheels were constructed with paddles or shallow buckets fixed at regular intervals around the circumference of the wheel. The water was directed to fill the buckets and, as they were filled, the weight of water forced the waterwheel to revolve. As the wheel turned on its upward journey, the buckets, now upside down, emptied, ready to repeat the filling process. Thus the wheel revolved and supplied power to the mill machinery. This was accomplished in one of two ways. In the first case, a slow-turning shaft ran from the axle of the waterwheel and its cog teeth meshed with much smaller cogs on a second rotating shaft which ran into the machine-house of the mill. This was called the line shaft. Since its cogs were much smaller than those of the axle shaft, they revolved much faster, and supplied the revolutions necessary to drive the machinery at high speeds. For one revolution of the waterwheel the line shaft would revolve many times more. The mill machinery was linked directly to the line shaft pulleys via leather or canvas belts.

Where a waterwheel was positioned lower than the bed of the mill-goit, stream or river, the water was channelled so as to fall on to the top of the waterwheel paddles. This was called a low-breast or overshot waterwheel, and is illustrated below. As stated, of the two types of wheel, the overshot waterwheel was the more efficient.

Richard Arkwright was one of many who benefited from John Smeaton's waterwheel design, the principle of which was carried through to the early nineteenth century.

Due to waterwheels generating so much dampness, waterwheels were often located outside the mill building.

Freezing temperatures could often cause problems, either by the flow of water being frozen or else the waterwheel itself being frozen, thus bringing mill production to a grinding halt.

The potential power of water is so often unrealised, certainly underrated, until it floods habitats, drowning houses and animals, and sweeping everything before it. Even worse still is to experience the terrifying and uncontrollable domination and noise of water in all its wild cruel savagery. Yet the commerce of cotton may never have flourished so rapidly without the advancement and efficiency in the use of the waterwheel in harnessing this force to provide the power to drive the machines in the mills and factories. An abundant supply of water was also an essential element for dye works, processing plants and print works. The demand for water had reached new heights. The North of England and Scotland were able to fulfil those demands due to the many streams, burns, and rivers, all thankfully fed by a continuous high rainfall.

Where once it was the weaver's cottage that had formed separate tiny factories for the weaving of cotton, enterprising merchants, the soon-to-be-rich mill-owners of the textile industry with Queen Cotton again taking the lead, began to move rapidly towards the

Water-wheel, overshot

Right and below: Overshot and undershot waterwheels. Where a waterwheel was positioned rather higher than the bed of the Goit, the waterwheel was constructed so that the water flowed directly over the paddles at approximately 9 o'clock, as shown below, on an undershot waterwheel.

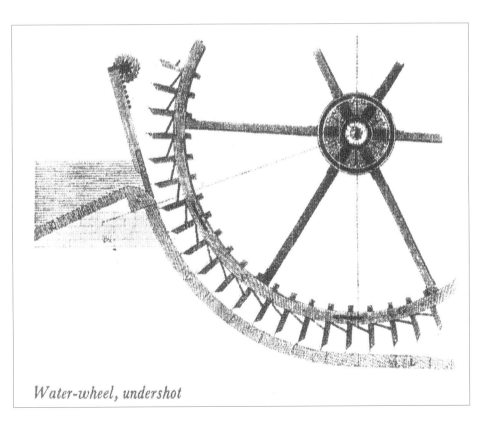

Water-wheel, undershot

gushing, babbling streams of the Pennines and the Northern Derbyshire Hills of England. Yet the weavers of the cottage industry had no need to fear for their jobs: their skills had, for over a century, kept starvation from their doors, and nothing was going to change now, for their experience was to be in great demand from the early mill-owners. An equally important Northern inheritance was the damp atmosphere, which was an essential requirement for the future spinning and weaving of the cotton. Thus began the growth of the cotton mills of England. Queen Cotton had arrived, as had the growing town of Manchester, which became know as 'The capital cotton town of England'. Indeed, Disraeli once described Manchester in its heyday as 'as great a human exploit as Athens'. By 1830, there were over 560 cotton mills in Lancashire employing more than 110,000 workers, of which 35,000 were children who were paid around 2s (approximately 11½p) per week, but the arrival of cotton also encouraged the birth of many smaller cotton towns such as Glossop, in Derbyshire, and numerous other villages throughout the North of England. The cotton revolution brought many changes: Manchester's population alone increased from 20,101 in 1700 to 48,821 in 1788. A further increase, supported by an employment invasion, raised it in 1838 to a staggering total of 181,708 people.

People were on the move, goods were on the move, roads made for the pack mule and pack horse mode of transport were outdated and unserviceable. New roads had to be constructed to cater for the wheeled transport of wagons and coaches propelled by teams of horses. Improvement of the road network was a vital requirement for progression of the Industrial Revolution. The answer lay in the introduction in 1706, of Turnpike Roads, administered by Turnpike Trusts. Use of a turnpike road was only permissible by paying a toll fee to the toll-keeper at a toll booth usually attached to the toll-keeper's house; many still stand now as private residences along country roads. By the 1750s most roads had been improved, and by the 1830s 20,000 miles of road were controlled by Turnpike Trusts, with tolls worth £1.5 million per annum. In 1754, the first stagecoach from Manchester to London began to operate and, barring accidents, the journey would take an uncomfortable four-and-a-half days to complete. The enhancement of harder, longer-lasting, serviceable roads was due to men like Metcalf, Telford and McAdam, who all played a crucial part in this essential progression.

With the growth of cotton mills, bales of raw cotton had to be transported from the delivery ports in America, via Liverpool, to the cotton mill towns of the North of England.

Horse-drawn transport was expensive, and numerous slow-flowing rivers in England became the main conveyance for heavy goods. Canals were being built, opening up new areas and improving the movement of coal and iron to the Northern industrial towns. The introduction of railways moved goods quickly by steam locomotive but, as trains needed huge amounts of coal and iron, canals helped provide cheaper transport.

The railway through the Longdendale Valley, commenced in 1839, was completed in 1845, providing the first rail link between Manchester and Sheffield. With railway stations at Hadfield, Crowden and Woodhead, and a link line to Glossop, this cultivated the transport system which was to benefit the Longdendale and Glossop mills. With Glossop being within 14 miles of Manchester's town centre, small towns and villages in the surrounding area were able to take full advantage of the allied business community. The cotton manufacturers, merchants, and mill-owners had already surrounded themselves with the hum and bustle of Manchester's magnificent new Cotton Exchange, which opened in 1729 and is still standing today, housing within its giant portals the Manchester Exchange Theatre – it is well worth a visit. In the area surrounding the Cotton Exchange, many huge stone cotton warehouses mushroomed, which have long since been converted into office accommodation and hotels. Years earlier, many coffee-houses in the

Market Place area of the town were the cotton-owners' meeting places, where much of the cotton trading business and bargaining was concluded.

About the year 1760, a considerable share of the calico-printing business was transferred from London to the North of England, where huge savings on production costs could be made due to the lower wages of the workforce coupled with cheaper accommodation costs – not unlike today. This transfer of business resulted in a fall in the price of cotton, and this, in turn, increased the demand for calicoes from the domestic markets. These goods, at that time, were made of linen warp and cotton weft, as it was difficult, before Sir Richard Arkwright's discovery, to spin fine cotton warp of sufficient strength without breaking. During the independent cottage factory days the dealers from Manchester, instead of buying fustians and calicoes from the weaver, as they had done previously, began to supply the weaver with all the necessary materials for the cloth – both the linen warp, and a portion of cotton wool which the weaver was obliged to use to complete the order. For this deal the weaver was paid a fixed price by the middleman, who was called a 'putter-out', working on behalf of the merchant. Weavers and winders would deliver their work to the putter-out and receive fresh material from him. The putter-out was responsible for guarding against theft and wastage and ensuring delivery days were met on time to keep the merchant's customers happy, but problems were normally solved in an amicable way. If the work was really faulty, the weaver was shown the fault and, if it was not a serious one, a caution would be admonished against repeating it. If the length or the weight was not as it should be, the weaver was informed, and the putter-out was expected to set it right at no extra cost to the merchant. If defaults persisted the weaver would no longer be employed by that particular merchant.

By now, so fast was the weaving of the finished goods outstripping the process of spinning the cotton, it frequently happened that the sum of money the master-weaver was paid by the putter-out was less than what the weaver paid to the spinner, already employed to spin the yarn. The weaver dare not complain to the spinner about the price, lest his looms should be unemployed.

Considering that the average master-weaver required at least six to seven spinners to keep him supplied with yarn, if this affair had continued the manufacture of the finished goods would have slowed to a grinding halt or, at least, many looms would become unemployed. Quicker spinning methods were now essential for, at that time, the only spinning machine known in England was the one-thread wheel. To have kept pace with the rate of weaving, if that was possible, would have meant training double the amount of spinners, to keep up with the skilled weavers. It was clear that a change in the system was necessary if the cotton industry was to meet this impending disaster. In 1760, about 800 tons of cotton was imported and used in British mills. By 1800, this figure had increased to 25,000 tons. Similarly, production of coal in Great Britain in 1800 was 6 million tons, compared to 23 million tons in 1830. Who was buying all these great quantities of coal, iron and cotton goods? None other than the textile industry, of course. They were the indirect buyer of huge quantities of coal including iron for making new machinery, and the direct purchaser of coal to provide steam power to drive it.

While the transport of coal and iron was becoming possible on a large scale, the textile industry was adapting those methods which had benefited both the coal and iron industry. It was in the newer cotton business that the textile inventions made most headway, because the older, established, and more prosperous, woollen trade was more conservative – it was, likewise, slower to move. The first steam-powered engines were invented in 1776 by a Scottish inventor and mechanical engineer, James Watt, jointly with a Birmingham businessman, Matthew Boulton, who had propounded a collection of small businesses and organised them together in one complex in Soho, Birmingham – the Soho Manufactory. Matthew encouraged Watt and supported him with cash to eventually capture the market from pumping water out of lead and coal mines. The partnership went on to develop the steam engine to fulfil the necessary arrangements to drive the machinery of the cotton industry.

Fortunately, different ingenious individuals had already begun to employ themselves in the art of contriving to improve on the simple spinning-wheel through implementing new and dextrous methods of spinning cotton. The race was on for inventors to speed up production; the cottage spinning wheel now being considered ponderous and laborious. Although the spinning and weaving of cotton into clothes by hand had gone on for centuries, it was in England in the mid-1700s that inventors developed textile machinery that was to revolutionise cotton manufacture and provide the impetus for the British Industrial Revolution that was to spread to America and throughout the world.

The Industrial Revolution left Great Britain as the most powerful nation on earth.

III

BRILLIANT INVENTORS SERVING QUEEN COTTON

The era of inventions was heralded in 1733, when John Kay, of Bury, created his earliest weaving machine with a flying shuttle (from which it derived its name). Weaving is the process of interlacing two or more sets of yarn at right angles to each other, with one set running in lengthways directions called the warp or filling, and the other length of yarn inserted crossways, called the weft. Long before Kay's time, a device had enabled the weaver to raise every alternative thread of his warp, so making a lane through which the shuttle with the weft thread could be passed, after which the alternative warp threads could be raised and the weft thread passed again so that the weft was actually woven in and out of the warp. If the cloth was wider than the span of a man's arm, an assistant had to be employed, standing at the opposite end of the loom, to return the shuttle. Kay's invention enabled the weaver to throw his shuttle through the warp and to return it to his hand by jerking a thread using one hand only. It doubled the work rate that one man could achieve, made wider cloth possible, and dispensed with the services of an assistant. This mechanical device was one of the most important advances in the art of weaving but, on hearing of the invention, and fearing for their jobs, a mob broke into Kay's house and destroyed the first machines. The opposition to new methods in England was so intense it forced Kay to emigrate to France and seek the protection of the French Government, who readily agreed, knowing their cotton industry would reap some benefits by their sponsorship. Undeterred, Kay doggedly worked on and, by 1750, had perfected his 'Flying Shuttle', as it became known, to actually double the work that one man could produce on the loom, which, in turn, increased the need for yarn.

Another unexpected benefit to France was the failure of Bonnie Prince Charlie to recover the British throne for the Roman Catholic Church in 1746, when he was defeated by the Duke of Cumberland at Culloden. A certain Jacobite manufacturer from Manchester, by the name of John Holker, fled to France and convinced both merchants and officials there of the desirability of using and stealing English and Scottish techniques for dyeing and printing textiles. For services rendered through these Machiavellian tendencies, he was allowed to build a factory in the Rouen suburb of Saint-Sever in the Seine Valley. Many of his imaginative products were carried via the slave vessels.

Spinning and weaving are inseparable in their relationship to supply and demand, and equanimity can only hope to be achieved when the amount of yarn required by the weaver equals the amount which the spinner can supply. This equilibrium could only be attained by inventors chasing their ideas on an even higher level as invention succeeded invention. As Kay's 'Flying Shuttle' doubled the amount of cloth that a weaver could produce, the demand for yarn increased, and this was fulfilled some years later when Lewis Paul and John Wyatt announced their device of spinning by rollers, a method by which the thread, as it was spun, was both drawn and twisted at the same time. Their idea did not come into general use until around 1760. It is usually difficult to pinpoint the actual year of inventions, as mill-owners were loath to take advantage of, or even admit to committing themselves to, new methods of production. Paul and Wyatt's germ of an idea – the drawing out and twisting threads in one operation – still exists in the present-day system. Also in 1760, improvements had begun to emerge in the carding process.

With Kay's machine already adding to the woes of the weavers, still more invention was necessary to find the balance in production of spinning and weaving propagated by John Kay's 'Flying Shuttle'.

This came by the inventiveness of James Hargreaves of Stanhill, near Church, Lancashire – a simple weaver without any mechanical knowledge who, in 1764, brilliantly created the 'Spinning Jenny', which he named after his wife. The idea for this machine was contrived one day when Hargreaves saw a common spinning machine being accidentally overturned. The wheel continued to revolve and work as it lay on the ground, and a new idea dawned. Through this invention, first patented in 1770, a person was able to double their work, with more ease than hand-carding. It gave the means of spinning twenty or thirty threads at once with no more labour than had previously been required to spin a single thread. The thread spun by the 'Jenny' could not, however, be used (except as weft), lacking the firmness and hardness required in the lengthwise threads. He adapted (and greatly improved) the stock cards used in the wool industry to the carding of cotton. In the stock cards, one of the cards is fixed while the other is suspended by a card over a pulley, which is worked by the carder. Using this method, two or even three cards can be directed to the same stock. Hargreaves' 'Spinning Jenny' was a wheel which turned, initially, eight spindles and then, later, sixteen spindles, as opposed to the previous single spindle which the hand-carder had used.

The 'Jenny' twisted the thread, and then returned it to the spindles again during the winding on of the yarn. During his early attempt at producing a rudely constructed 'Jenny' of eight spindles, a mob broke into his house and destroyed the machine. Some time later, when the advantages of the 'Jenny' were common knowledge, carders and spinners, fearing their livelihood would be taken from them, rose a second time and, scouring the country, broke every carding and spinning machine they could find. In a very short time the 'Jenny' put an end to the spinning of cotton by the common wheel, and the whole operation of spinning cotton was accomplished by this machine. When the 'Jenny' was finally patented by Hargreaves in 1780, the structure of his machine had greatly improved, eventually operating as many as eighty spindles. Spin-off followed spin-off, and Hargreaves' invention of 1764 inspired another man, Richard Arkwright, to invent the 'Spinning Frame', a spinning machine powered by water that produced a cotton yarn suitable for warp (lengthwise threads) – an improvement on James Hargreaves' 'Spinning Jenny', which produced a coarse, weaker thread used only for the filling or weft (crossways threads).

One of the greatest cotton machine inventors of his day was Richard Arkwright, who was born in Preston, Lancashire, on 23 December 1732. He was the youngest of thirteen children, and from a working-class family. His first wife, Patience, bore him a son, Richard, but sadly Patience died less than a year later. In 1761, he married his second wife, Margaret, with whom he had a daughter, Susanna. In 1760, he established himself in Bolton-le-Moor as a barber and he developed his business potential by becoming a wigmaker and merchant. He discovered a valuable chemical process for dyeing hair, and the profits he earned were used to purchase property. He became landlord of the Black Boy public house in 1762.

His friend John Kay (no relation to the Kay who invented the 'Flying Shuttle'), a local watchmaker from Warrington, encouraged him to take an interest in mechanical engineering. Working in a thriving industrial area, Arkwright enabled himself to become acquainted with the various cotton techniques. In about 1767, together with Kay, who became his mechanic, and some friends, John Smalley and David Thornley, he rented a room in the parlour of a house belonging to the Free Grammar School at Preston. The room of the house was secluded behind some gooseberry bushes, and they were so secretive that the neighbours were suspicious and accused them of sorcery. Two old ladies complained that the humming sounds emitted from the house at night must be the devil tuning his bagpipes. His inventions resulted in the 'Spinning Frame', which enabled cotton to be drawn out and spun much quicker and, more importantly, to be spun to a high degree of fineness with far fewer production stoppages. It was no doubt a brilliant invention, and he is quoted as saying that the inspiration for his invention was seeing a red hot iron bar being elongated by being passed through a series of rollers. The actual date of his invention is unknown but it is generally assumed to be about 1768 for, in 1769, he obtained his patent for spinning with rollers. 'The Spinning Frame', as it was first called, was too heavy to be operated by hand and, after further experimenting by trial and error, it was successfully driven by water power. The name was later changed to the 'Throstle' once it had become fully developed. The word 'throstle' is a British term for all spinning machines because the noise of the machine when operating resembles the note of the throstle or thrush. When operated, it performed in itself the whole process of spinning, leaving only the weaver the task of supplying the prepared material and of joining or piecing the thread when it breaks – without question, a breakthrough invention. To avoid an attack by the same lawless rabble that had driven Hargreaves out of Lancashire, they moved, in 1768, to Nottingham, where his inventiveness was frustrated by a lack of capital. In the year of his death, a visitor to Ashton-under-Lyne wrote in his diary: 'It is very curious and surprising to see the spinning mules and jennies, as they call them, spin off 144 threads at once. They spin one pound of cotton to so fine a thread that it will reach 95 miles and a half.' Now that would have brought a smile of satisfaction to Sir Richard's face.

In an attempt to remedy the situation, the shrewd Arkwright invited a Mr Strutt, of Derby, who was mainly a stocking manufacture experienced in mechanical engineering, together with Strutt's business partner, Mr Need, to see for themselves Arkwright's latest inventions. Satisfying themselves of the Spinning Frame's great potential, they immediately went into partnership with Arkwright. Armed with the right financial requirements, in 1769, Arkwright was able to erect his first mill at Nottingham driven by horse power; he also took out a further patent for spinning by rollers.

Finding that horse power was too expensive, they moved to Cromford, Derbyshire, in 1771, where they built the first water-powered spinning mill. Cromford possessed Bonsall Brook, a good swift stream abounding with water that flowed into the river Derwent half a mile downstream. This provided the forceful water power required to drive his heavy 'Water Frame'. A year later he built Masson Mill, a large mill of six storeys.

Also flowing into Bonsall Brook is Cromford Sough, which is a drain from the lead mines under the hillside, together with some hot springs which helped to keep the water to the millrace warm all the year round (and therefore free from freezing), ensuring a reliable water-powered supply. Arkwright raised the levels of both the Sough and Bonsall Brook so that John

Smeaton's overshot wheels gave him enough power to operate his much later larger spinning frames, capable of operating 256 spindles. The waterwheels at Cromford have long gone, but still to be seen are the massive bed stones where the bearings once rested, as well as marks on the masonry scarred long ago by the revolving waterwheels.

One of Arkwright's original Water Frames is still in working order at the Helmshore Museum, Cromford, powered today by electricity, a far cry from the days of water power.

Cromford became known as the 'Cradle of the Industrial Revolution' and, within two years of mills using Arkwright's Water Frame under licence, 180 cotton mills had sprung up and England became dotted with textile plants. On the introduction of steam power by James Watt, Arkwright used the new steam engine to power his machines at his new factories in Lancashire, Scotland and Staffordshire, further amassing his fortune. Understandably, Arkwright had many enemies amongst his business competitors, for they considered him unscrupulous in adopting other people's ideas. One described Arkwright as a thickset man with cunning lips. Partly because of this, but more because they feared they would suffer financially, Arkwright was able to retain his precious patent rights until 1772, when his adversaries eventually contested the patents entitlements of his invention. The matter went to litigation, but a verdict was given in Arkwright's favour.

After his removal to Cromford, Arkwright followed up with other inventions for preparing the cotton for spinning, and he took out a fresh patent in the year 1775. The exclusive use of his inventions remained undisturbed for a further six years until, in 1781, his rights to this patent were disputed, and final judgement was given against him in the Court of Kings Bench in November 1785. His patent was cancelled, and manufacturers were permitted to copy his design. He never again matched the first brilliant ideas of his genius. Arkwright's style of management, his eye for detail, and the systematic way he arranged and programmed his departments and machines were copied by many others. Indeed, it is fair to say that few basic cotton mill layouts have been improved, or even equalled, since Richard Arkwright's brilliant accomplishments.

Arkwright's mills worked almost twenty-three hours a day from 6 a.m., with a thirty-minute breakfast break and a forty-minute lunch break. There is no doubt that Arkwright's inventions opened up new and boundless fields of employment which brought real benefit to Britain. Arkwright was one of the first businessmen to realise that by keeping your workforce happy greater were the chances of increasing production. To this end, he attended to their welfare at his Cromford Mill, just south of Matlock Bath, Derbyshire. He built new homes for his workers in the village of Cromford, transforming a scattered community of lead-working families into a tightly knit cotton community. He was the father of the factory system, and is recognised as one of the world's first great industrialists, a hard-headed businessman with a soft heart for human kindness. He was High Sheriff of Derbyshire in 1786, and was knighted in the same year by King George III for his contribution to British industry, and for opening up a new fields of employment. Loved and respected by his workers, Sir Richard Arkwright died in 1792, at the age of sixty, at his works in Cromford. First buried at the Parish Church, on the completion of Cromford Church he was reburied there.

Not all of the cotton industry inventors fared so well as Arkwright. For example, the gentle Bolton-born Samuel Crompton, with his fine emaciated profile, worked from his father's house, perfecting his brainchild, 'The Mule'. This was a much improved version of Hargreaves' 'Spinning Jenny', and was one of the most important machines ever offered to the cotton industry. It was a means of combining a finesse of thread with great strength beyond their wildest dreams. Industrial spies, realising by now the fortune-making potential of improving the production of cotton, actually bored spy holes through Crompton's wall, and at night they would put up ladders against the windows in an attempt to learn more.

Supplementary waterwheel at Cromford Mill. Diameter of 18ft, and 7ft wide. The main wheel was reputed to be 25ft in diameter and 12ft wide.

Mill hands operating Crompton's 'Spinning Mule'. (Courtesy of Edward Baines' book, *History of the Cotton Manufacture in Great Britain*, published in 1835)

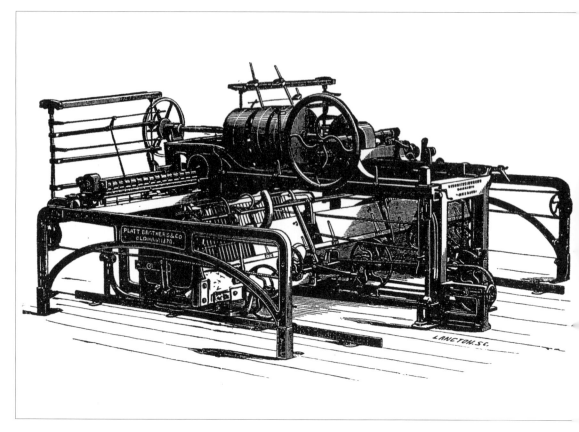

'Hand Mule' – hand-operated spinning machine.

At last, in 1775, after years of hard work, Crompton perfected his 'Spinning Mule'. The proud, honest-thinking Crompton, unlike Arkwright, lacked business acumen, and openly revealed his invention to his supposed cotton business friends. They used him, and the 'Spinning Mule', to make huge profits, promising the trusting Crompton that, given time, he would receive royalties galore from his invention.

Crompton was swindled; for the advantages of his 'Mule' did not come into general use, nor was its value known, until after the expiration of Arkwright's patent.

The meagre recompense this great inventor received for his contribution to the supremacy of British manufactures was inadequate and unrewarding. After working fastidiously all his life, Samuel Crompton, born 1753, died in 1827 in comparative poverty at his home in King Street, Bolton, and was buried in St Peter's Church.

Robert and Thomas Barber had patented an original power-loom in 1774, but it was Edmund Cartwright, another English inventor, who devised the first water and steam-driven power-loom of real significance. He was born in Marnham, Nottinghamshire, in 1743, and educated at Wakefield Grammar School, Nottinghamshire, from where he progressed to University College, Oxford. In 1764, he was elected to a fellowship at Magdalen, before deciding to become a rector at Marwood in 1779. He would probably have remained a country rector had he not happened to be in Matlock in the summer of 1784, and entered into conversation with a gentleman from

Manchester, who began talking about Richard Arkwright's spinning machine. The Manchester gentleman predicted that, once Arkwright's patent had expired, there would be a surplus of spun cotton, with never enough weavers to keep up with the spinning production. This chance conversation resulted in Cartwright inventing what he himself admitted was 'a most rude piece of machinery', which was then patented in 1785. He kept on improving his design until 1787, when he satisfied himself he had developed it into the modern power-loom of his day. Only then did he take out his final patent.

Imitating others, Revd Cartwright realised the potential of his invention and soon became a manufacturer, with cotton mills in Doncaster. Eight years later, this had proved a financial failure. In 1791, another of his mills in Manchester was wilfully destroyed by fire, but Cartwright doggedly pressed on and, in 1789, he patented a wool-combing machine for which he took out patents in 1790 and 1792. Once again these efforts were a failure financially. After attempting a variety of new inventions, which were never as successful as his power-loom, Cartwright became financially embarrassed. Fortunately for him, Parliament awarded him £10,000 for the benefits that Britain had received from his successful power-loom invention, and this was at last proved and recognised throughout the cotton industry. He bought a small farm in Sevenoaks, Kent, where, although retired, he continued to invent various agricultural implements. Revd Cartwright, as he was always known, died in Hastings on 30 October 1823.

Yet change was piecemeal, and was not accomplished without a fight. In many areas inventions spread slowly and unevenly. Between 1760 and 1830 there was an enormous increase in cotton production, yet it is hard to believe that, in 1830, there were an estimated 240,000 hand-looms still being used, as against only 60,000 power-looms, even though spinning was almost a steam-powered factory operation. It was cheaper to use water power than steam power, and many mills only added steam power to provide power in an emergency, or for backup in times of drought. Mill-owners still met with fierce resistance when attempting to modernise their factories and mills, and this was clearly demonstrated by the reactions of the Luddites.

Spinning and weaving again drew level, and a new equilibrium was achieved, aided by the use of new steam and turbine power to drive the machinery and of new materials in its manufacture, resulting in a huge increase in production of goods both for the home market and the overseas trade. With this assurance, Manchester built a magnificent stone Cotton Warehouse in 1856, specialising in the wholesale selling of drapery. After laying derelict for a number of years, the warehouse was renovated completely, and is now the imposing and distinguished Britannia Hotel. There is no doubt that the combined inventions of all those ingenious men opened up new and boundless fields of employment, bringing great benefit to the cotton industry and the British nation.

The engineers and inventors were mostly pragmatic, self-educated men like Hargreaves and Crompton, possessing practical craftsmanship. In the welter of fortune-making, the inventor rarely prospered as much as the businessman, yet there was a general difference between the two types. Arkwright stands out as typical of the unscrupulous, self-made entrepreneurs who exploited other people's ideas, and combined this with leadership and business acumen. Conversely, we have Crompton, the inventor of the 'Mule', who represents the other type of inventor, with little business flair. A French historian comparing the portraits of the two men said courtly: 'Arkwright, with his fat vulgar face, his goggling heavy lidded eyes, the vigorous line of the brow, the cunning lips, then there was the contrasting Crompton, with his refined and emaciated profile, his fine forehead, the austere line of his mouth. Together these men represent invention and industry, the genius which creates revolutions and the power which possesses itself with results.'

Inventors played a huge part in the progression of the Industrial Revolution, most of them prospered and certainly many other people made fortunes by their efforts. As the giant textile industry expanded, so the importance of the inventors grew, and later in the century those same inventors moulded the policy of state and went on to attain political power beyond their wildest expectations. In the North West of England cotton dominated the textile industry and gained the proud title: 'Clothier of the World'.

IV

PRINCIPAL MACHINES IN THE AGE OF COTTON

Cotton must be spun into yarn before it can be made into cloth, and there are three main stages before this operation can be accomplished – carding, spinning, and weaving. Spinning cannot begin until after the raw fibre has been cleaned and carded, so the first machines used are the Opener and Scutcher Machines, employed in the process of cleaning the raw cotton and separating its matted flock. The Lap Machine then fashions the raw cotton into flat folds. In the Carding Engine (or Machine) it is carded and further cleaned, and the fibres straightened, making it easier to spin. Next come the Combing and Drawing Frames, where the raw cotton is formed into a loose rope, the fibres of which are laid parallel, followed by the Slubbing Frame, where it is slightly twisted. The Throttle Frame is chiefly used for coarse wraps, and upon the Self Acting and Hand Mules, both coarse and fine yarns are spun. On completion of this operation the spun cotton is now ready to be turned into cloth using weaving machines.

The first stage is in the Opening or Blowing Room, where bales of raw cotton are opened and the raw cotton is spread uniformly on a feeding table then fed into a cylindrical beater which spins at 1,400rpm. After beating, a strong draught of fresh air is made to play through the newly opened cotton, reducing the matted flocks it possessed. By means of an ingenious contraption, a strong draught of air is made to play through the newly opened cotton, cleaning and carrying away the dust, foreign particles and vegetable matter which adhere to it. Lord Brothers Opener Machine, as illustrated on the following pages, possessed a sequence for drawing the cotton, by means of a vacuum, from places situated at long distances from the Blowing Room.

Carding partially aligns the fibres and forms them into a thin web that is brought together as a soft, very weak rope of fibres called a 'carded sliver'. From the Lap Machine the raw cotton is passed on to the Carding Engine, which consists of one large or main cylinder covered with cards, a smaller one called the 'doffer', and a still smaller one called called the 'taker in'. The main cylinder is surmounted with small ones, called rollers, covered in a similar manner with cards, by whose revolutions, in the opposite direction to those of the larger cylinder and with different velocities, the cotton is carded and put on the second cylinder or 'doffer'. The third cylinder, or 'taker in', is usually covered with a stronger wire, it receives the cotton from a pair of feed roller-skates, striking out the heavier part of the dirt remaining from the scrutcher and delivering the cotton to the main cylinder where it is further carded, cleaned, and the fibres straightened, in the Combing Machine before progressing to the Drawing Frame.

Lord Brothers Opener Machine, employed in the process of cleaning raw cotton.

Single Scutcher and Lap Machine. The combination of Scutcher and Lap Machine clean the cotton further and carry it forward in the same manner as the Opener, making laps for the Second/Finishing Scutcher, which separates the fibres and fashions it into flat folds.

Combined Opener, Beater, and Lap Machine. A combined three-cylinder Opener, Beater, Finishing Scutcher, and Lap Machine.

Self-Stripping Flat Carding Machine.

Combing Machine – further removes tangles from the cotton fibres.

Drawing Frame. In the Drawing Frame, the process of elongation is carried out and the raw cotton is formed into a loose rope, the fibres of which are laid parallel, before being transferred to the Slubbing Frame. Drawing out increases the parallelism of the fibres and combines several carded slivers into one 'drawn sliver', or continuous strand of cotton.

The Slubbing Frame. The operation which succeeds that of the Drawing Frame is slubbing, where the sliver has a certain amount of twist imparted to it, and is wound on a bobbin. In the Slubbing Frame, the still raw cotton goes through part of an interesting system where, as the bobbins fill and increase in diameter, their rate is gradually made slower at each layer by an ingenious device known as 'the sun and planet motion'. Thus, the Slubbing Frame serves three purposes: (a) it draws out the cotton using rollers; (b) then spindles twist it; (c) it winds the cotton into a bobbin by the flyers and pressers before being further processed in the Intermediate and Finishing Frames, where it is twisted still further, particularly in the higher numbers. However, it is not yet yarn.

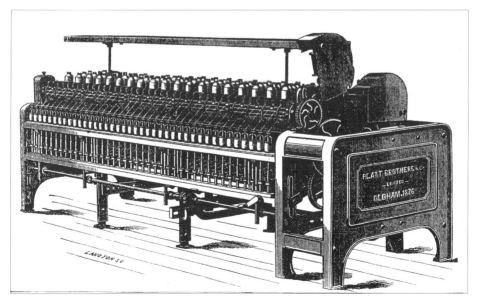

The Throstle Frame. The roving process reduces the drawn sliver, increases the parallel alignment of the fibres, and inserts a small amount of twist in the strand, now known as roving. The number of spindles commonly put into the throstle is from 100 to 150 on each side. The Throstle Frame is chiefly used for coarse wraps which differ from the self-acting and hand-mules.

Self-Acting Mule (power-driven).

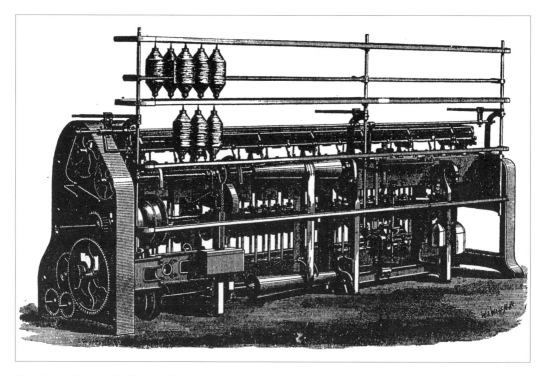

The Roving Frame. The Roving Frame performs the last requirement before the operation of spinning, and resembles, in principle, the Slubbing and Intermediate Frames. It has a greater number of spindles than either, seldom less than 100, and often 164; these spindles are set closer together, and the bobbins are shorter and smaller than in the Intermediate Frame.

In 1818, William Elton obtained a patent in which the operations normally performed by a spinner were made automatic and, although not extensively adapted, contained several ingenious arrangements to improve the machine's performance. Mr Smith of Deanston, Scotland, also contributed to this machine. Then, in around 1824, Richard Roberts directed his ideas into rendering the 'Mule' self-acting, both in 1825 and 1830, when he took out further patents by adding his 'quadrant' winding apparatus, which rewinds the yarn from spools to spools or cones, thus completing this 'Self-Acting Mule', adding further chapters to the genius of all the inventors of machines in the cotton industry. These great Victorian inventors helped Britain to become the most productive and richest cotton country on the planet.

The mill-owners who speculated with these new methods of production obtained profits far exceeding the wildest dreams of earlier generations, and were mostly men with a highly developed grasping instinct. Others would describe them as men of vision. Often these penniless entrepreneurs were able to exploit wealthy partners willing to link their wealth and business acumen with the entrepreneur's own predisposition to genius. A good example of a self-made entrepreneur was Robert Owen, the son of a saddler and ironmonger, who was apprenticed to a draper in Stamford. At the age of twenty he became manager of one of Manchester's largest factories, before setting up as an independent cotton spinner. He began with only three cotton hands, but went on to become one of the most successful mill-owners in the extensive and lucrative Scottish cotton mills of Lanark. From observations as cotton master in his own cotton mills, he went on to become a great social reformer in the battle against child labour.

V

ELI WHITNEY —
AMERICAN GIN MILL INVENTOR

Eli Whitney was a Law graduate from Yale University who, like many university graduates of today, had large debts which had to be repaid: Eli required a job fast. On finding a post as a tutor to the children of Catherine Brown, a cotton plantation owner in South Carolina, he reluctantly left his New England home in Massachusetts, and travelled south to take up his new appointment. Without realising the profound effect the next seven months would have on his life, Eli soon acquainted himself with the tedious and arduous task performed by the black plantation slaves, of removing by hand the cotton-seed from the fibre. Catherine Brown encouraged Eli to find a solution to this time-consuming problem, so he put aside his previous ambition of becoming a lawyer and devoted himself to this burning question. The fact remained — mechanisation of spinning in England had created a greatly expanded market on the cotton front, and it was little wonder this expanded American trade had created a bottleneck in the removal of the seeds from the raw cotton fibre. Spending a whole winter and the following spring in a secret workshop provided by Catherine, he at last developed and created the first Gin Mill.

The Gin Mill worked by first pulling the cotton through a set of wire teeth mounted on a revolving cylinder, so that the fibre passed through narrow slots in an iron breastwork too small to permit the passage of the seed. Eli patented his invention, even though it was, at this stage, simply hand-cranked. He later developed versions of his Gin Mill which could be harnessed to a horse or driven by water power. Eli Whitney had eliminated the task of removing the seed from the fibre by hand (which had, up until then, been done by the black plantation slaves). Following the invention of Whitney's Cotton Gin in 1793 (the same year in which the existence of six slave states in America was recorded) the yield of raw cotton doubled, and, by mid-century, America was growing three-quarters of the world's supply of cotton, most of it being shipped to Manchester, England, via Liverpool, to be manufactured into cloth.

Because of the simplicity of Eli Whitney's design, unscrupulous plantation owners copied his idea, and he made little profit from the Gin Mill invention which had made him so famous. He struggled to make a profit, weighed down with legal battles. Unfortunately for Eli his aspiring hopes of reducing slavery failed. The plantation owners' greed for bigger profits only increased their demand for more and more slave labour to grow and pick their cotton.

Eli Whitney's Gin Mill.

Eli Whitney's 'Stand of Arms'.

But Eli Whitney ultimately triumphed. He invented a way of manufacturing 'a stand of arms' by machine, so that the parts were interchangeable. A stand of arms included the musket, its bayonet and ramrod, all of which had to fit securely and smoothly on to the weapon, and be durable in use.

Whitney himself manufactured the necessary parts and, during the twelve years of his contract, supplied a total of 10,000 muskets to the Yankee Government. It helped the Northern States win the Civil War against the South and the principle of slave labour. Eli Whitney died a wealthy man in 1825.

VI

SLAVERY — THE TRADE
IN HUMAN SOULS

Fate deemed it that Queen Cotton and slavery were to spread woefully together – an unhealthy mix of Mother Nature and man. The first Negroes had been landed in the earliest colony of Virginia in 1621, coinciding with the first cotton plant being grown in the same year, and the first harvest of cotton being reaped twelve months later. At that time, Queen Cotton had not yet been recognised as such an immensely useful and versatile crop. She would enable cloth to be manufactured into clothes and a huge variety of other household goods, and so replace the heavy and expensive woollen commodities. It was not until 1775 that the cultivation of cotton began to take on such significance in America, overtaking in importance such other essential crops as rice and wheat, and even becoming more important than growing tobacco. An American apologist for slavery, addressing a British readership in 1863, wrote: 'The negro and the cotton plant seem to be natural allies and their almost simultaneous introduction into that part of the world now known as the Confederate States of America was a most fortunate circumstance for both the black and white race.' At the time of the Declaration of Independence in 1776, the existing fourteen states, including at that time the unnamed South West Territory, already possessed between them over 500,000 slaves, three-quarters of whom were concentrated in Virginia and North and South Carolina, and almost all of whom were in the South. By 1790, the total number of slaves had risen to 700,000, even though the number in the northern states had dropped considerably. The onslaught of raw cotton, shipped directly across the Atlantic Ocean, continued, arriving at the thriving seaport of Liverpool.

From 1700 to 1800, Liverpool was converted from a sleepy fishing village into one of the busiest slave-trading ports in the British Isles. Liverpool's first wet dock was commissioned by the borough council in 1709, was designed and constructed by Thomas Steers, and was officially opened in 1715 – this became known as the Old Dock. The Graving Docks (or dry docks) were built from 1756 to 1769, and were used to repair and clean the barnacles off the hulls of the slave-trading vessels.

Liverpool's expanding overseas trade demanded more shipping berths, so an Act of Parliament was granted for the construction of George Dock, together with a lighthouse and piers. George Dock was completed in 1771 and positioned at the foot of the present Water Street, now occupied by the Royal Liver Buildings. By 1788, King's Dock was opened, a year prior to the French Revolution, which further increased her exports. This was the dawning of the great dock complex which was once the great thriving, buzzing seaport of Liverpool. Between 1700 and 1790, sugar imports increased fivefold, rum and tobacco threefold, and cotton by fifty times. These imported increases resulted in the construction of Queen's Dock in 1796. Similarly, Liverpool exported shiploads of manufactured goods from Manchester, as well as firearms and gunpowder — enticing merchandise for the slave traders of Africa and the West Indies. Tons of raw cotton was landed in Liverpool and quickly transported conveniently to the warehouses of Manchester and to the cotton mills of Lancashire and Derbyshire, where the raw cotton was quickly woven.

Liverpool's first slave ship sailed in 1700. She was disdainfully named the *Blessing*. It is difficult to understand the thinking of such eminent so-called gentlemen of their day who looked upon slave trading as an honorable profession. In 1752, one such Liverpool slave trader was Richard Gildart, listed within the Company of Merchants trading in Africa. Gildart was a town councillor and mayor to the town on three occasions, a bailiff, and MP for Liverpool from 1734–1754. He owned at least three slave ships, and they named a street after him. In 1753, only four rich families had private carriages in Liverpool — three of them were slave merchants.

Jamaica was the largest British colony in the West Indies and, in 1655, became a major source of sugar. Many of the merchants had sugar plantations and lived on their own estates. These same merchants were soon to find a more lucrative form of business and became slave traders. Jamaica quickly became the target destination for many of Liverpool's slave ships, and three out of every four slaves shipped to Jamaica were transported in Liverpool vessels.

'In South Carolina, the slaves were well fed, well clothed, less worked, and never severely whipped. In Jamaica, they were badly fed, indifferently clothed, hard worked, and severely whipped.' So stated Captain Thomas Wilson of the British Navy, who had experienced both mainland America and the West Indies. He was giving evidence to the House of Commons in London — this was the attitude of middle Britain regarding slavery in 1790. Early in the eighteenth century, Liverpool was the main outlet for Manchester's manufactured merchandise, encouraged by low transport costs. Much of Lancashire's cotton goods, especially the coarse striped annabasses copied from India, and the outstanding manufactured cotton checks of Samuel Touchett, were exported to Africa and the West Indies in exchange for slaves. Samuel Touchett, who later became a Member of Parliament, was also an occasional slave merchant.

In 1730, the number of slave vessels sailing to Africa from Liverpool had increased to fifteen, and by 1799 134 ships sailed from the port. In 1737, one vessel, the *Lively*, was reported to have made a record-breaking profit of 300 per cent! By 1795, Liverpool had overtaken both Bristol and London in the importation and exportation of slaves. Between 1793 and 1808, 37,086 slaves per year had been imported to Liverpool in 135 ships, with over 5,000 slaving voyages leaving the port for Africa. Little wonder that, by 1780, the African slave trade appeared to be an essential part of both the British and American economies. Liverpool's giant growth during the eighteenth century was largely due to huge profits made in the African and West Indies slave trade and the import of sugar and rum, which brought an increasing demand for more storage space for bales of cotton and slaves in transit.

The merchants lost no time in building the famous Goree Warehouse on the dock front in 1793. They named it after Sengali's Goree Island off the coast of Africa, where the British had control of the most important anchorages in Africa. Thousands of Africans were captured there and transported to America and the West Indies via Liverpool, which was one reason for Liverpool's great increase in trade. Many slaves shipped across the triangular slave voyage would find themselves chained and shackled to each other beneath the huge, deep, cold, dark cellars of the Goree Warehouse before they continued their voyage of horror.

The most dominant abolitionist of his day was William Wilberforce MP (1759–1833), who was a master of diplomatic propaganda, and well qualified to lead the Parliamentary campaign to end

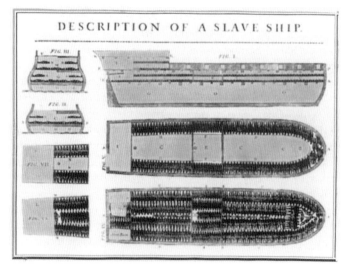

Plan of the Liverpool slave ship, *Brookes*. The above plan, together with a report of her barbarous activities, was first sponsored and published in 1789, by England's Abolitionist Society, when it was brought to the Society's attention that the vessel usually transported in her holds 600 or more slaves. Named after a Liverpool family and sailing from Liverpool to the Gold Coast the *Brookes* was legally allowed to carry 450 slaves; every dot on the plan represents a heart beating human being, totalling 609 men, women and children.

The Society distributed thousands of copies of the above diagram in a pamphlet reporting the suffering and unbearable conditions the slaves had to endure in being chained together tightly packed in oppressive heat, in a cauldron of filth, disease, human waste, vomit, beating, rape and heartache. The pamphlet was not only distributed to many prominent people including Members of Parliament, but also to newspapers, magazines, inns, pubs and reproduced on posters wherever there was space.

The British public's awareness and revulsion to the situation was to eventually end the sufferings of the greedy crimes of slavery. In 1804, the *Brookes* ended her cruel transport of slaves when she was held then confiscated by authorities in Buenos Aires and ended up in the dry dock of a breakers yard.

slavery. Together with Thomas Clarke and the Society for the Abolition of the Slave Trade, they were determined to continue the fight to end this vile practice.

Through its Quaker connections, the abolitionist movement against the slave trade became stronger, yet during a hearing of evidence at the bar of the House of Commons, as expected, the merchants from Liverpool did all they could to discredit the Bill, making the odious claim that not only were the ships transporting the slaves suitable, but the passage from Africa, with so much merrymaking on the deck, was one of the happiest periods of a Negro's life. An early milestone was reached in 1772, when the English courts decided, in the famous Somerset case, that a slave became free as soon as he set foot on English soil (although the last public sale of a black slave in England appears to have been on Liverpool's waterfront in 1779 – the import and export of slaves there continued).

The population of Liverpool in 1788 was 55,732, and that included approximately fifty black or mulatto boys and girls. They were not slaves, but children of African merchants sent to England to be educated. By this time the anti-slavery movement had awoken public opinion against all expectations, and one abolition movement in Liverpool even held public meetings on the dock front. Born in Mount Pleasant, Liverpool, in 1753, William Roscoe, lawyer and poet, the best-known Liverpool abolitionist, wrote pamphlets in favour of the abolition of slavery. One of his poems read:

Shame to mankind! but shame to Britons most,
Who all the sweets of liberty can boast,
Yet, deaf to every human claim deny
That bliss to others, which themselves enjoy.

Another Liverpool abolitionist was James Currie, and it is recorded that, at one dock-front public meeting, Currie was set upon by irritated merchants and thrown into the dock. Fortunately, his friend Roscoe rescued him. Roscoe lived to be seventy-eight years of age, and was buried in Roscoe Memorial Gardens, Liverpool, in 1831.

Manchester was thankful to receive the raw cotton that those very slaves had cruelly toiled to harvest, yet despite its interests in cheap raw imported cotton, two-thirds of Manchester's male population signed a petition demanding an end to the slave trade. Over 100 English towns followed their example, yet the Liverpool sail-makers expressed horror at the idea of an end to this traffic. Bitterness between the warring slave trade factions continued relentlessly, and it was not until 1807 that the slave trade was mercifully banned in Britain. Despite this, however, illegal slave trading continued for another sixty years. The United States abolition followed in 1808, but there too illegal trading continued in many Southern states.

Ironically, Queen Cotton had united Manchester to their neighbours Liverpool, but the anti-slavery laws had highlighted a not so friendly rivalry, which still exists today, in 'football red', between these two great Lancashire cities. The proud town of the Manchester gentlemen was surrounded by gargantuan stone cotton mills resembling industrial cathedrals, accompanied by 300ft-high brick chimneys. They were as numerous as the masts of the tall slave ships that stood silhouetted against the grey sky of Liverpool's dock land, inciting every Liverpool Lad not to see slave ships, but to view with pompous dignity their lofty, mysterious, majestic waterfront. Indeed, in 1849, Herman Melville described the scene in his novel *Moby Dick*, through the character Redburn: 'In magnitude, cost and durability, the docks of Liverpool surpass all others in the world, for miles you may walk along that riverside, passing dock after dock like a chain of immense fortresses.'

Manchester, being a landlocked cotton town, had to have all her goods delivered by road or rail to Liverpool docks in order to export abroad, with incoming goods being delivered by the same route. Liverpool charged prohibitive toll and harbour taxes, thus reducing the Mancunian gentlemen's profitability. They were not happy, but reluctantly accepted it, at the same time as the seed of an idea was emerging – the construction of their own gateway to the river Mersey: the Manchester Ship Canal. Liverpool continued to import cotton, Manchester continued to manufacture it, and both Liverpool and Manchester continued to prosper.

The last British slave ship recorded to have sailed from Liverpool left under Captain Hugh Crow, a Manxman, but slave trading continued into the 1890s to both Africa and the Americas.

With the collapse in the trade of human souls, there were, mercifully, no more chained slaves shuffling along Liverpool's waterfront. However, a new trade had emerged, in the shape of emigration. Instead of black people being packed into holds to be delivered to the Deep South, it was white people sailing to America to be landed at Ellis Island. Princes Dock was built in 1821, and named after Prince Regent, who was, incidentally, crowned King George IV on the day of its official opening. The Princes Dock was the largest ever constructed at that time and was the first dock to have a 5m-high stone boundary wall built around it – this was reputed, wrongly, to keep the slaves from escaping. However, by that time, thankfully, there were no more slaves to escape.

From the Princes Dock, a million emigrants sailed to America, including many families who were casualties from the demise of the cotton industry, all searching for a new beginning in that far-away open country of opportunity, America. Today, there are thirty-seven Manchesters and fifteen Liverpool townships in the USA. Who knows how many people now living in the United States have ancestors in the United Kingdom who walked down the gangplanks of those tall emigrant ships, sailing from Liverpool to the New World seeking their fortunes. One such Englishman was a man named Samuel Slater.

VII

A BRIT EMIGRATES TO AMERICA

Samuel Slater was born in Belper, in the county of Derbyshire in 1768, the son of William Slater, a wealthy landowner and speculator. By coincidence, Samuel was born in the same year Richard Arkwright invented his Spinning Frame and so, as Sam grew up, the British textile industry grew and expanded. In Samuel's youth, one of Richard Arkwright's business partners, Jedediah Strutt, contacted Samuel's father to buy land and the water rights from him to build a new cotton mill in Derbyshire; this relationship led to Strutt offering an apprenticeship to one of William's sons. Strutt had preferred Sam's eldest brother, William, but Samuel was chosen because of his age and competence in arithmetic. William (Snr) had enough faith in his son to pay for him to pursue the highest level of management training. During Samuel's apprenticeship he lived in Strutt's house. Unfortunately, during this period, Sam's father died in a farming accident, leaving all his sons a share in his inheritance. Sam's share remained untouched at the end of his apprenticeship. Sam spent seven years with Strutt and became his bookkeeper and right-hand man, thus putting Sam in the enviable position of learning and experiencing every aspect of management regarding the English cotton industry.

Sam also knew that the cotton industry in England was becoming overextended, and realised he could possibly make his fortune in America. Emigration was difficult at that time, for the British Government, in an effort to stop their skilled mechanics from sharing technology and machine design with foreign countries, had placed an embargo on free movement out of the United Kingdom. Today the Government places restrictions on many of those who desire to enter the country, and enforcement orders on those who enter illegally.

Since Richard Arkwright was noted for his unprincipled adoption of other people's ideas, Hargeaves' 'Spinning Jenny' being an example, it is ironic that, in England, the patent rights of Arkwright's own inventions were constantly being contested by his homeland adversaries. This knowledge, together with the overseas embargo, compelled the twenty-one-year-old Sam to tell no one about his plans, and, armed with his apprentice indenture papers, his managerial qualifications, and his smuggled drawings, he sneaked through English customs disguised as an agriculture worker. He landed on Ellis Island, New York, in November 1789. Sam promptly found a job in a small textile mill in the city and it was here that he learned of Moses Brown, the great Quaker merchant, who had resisted his brother's involvement in the slave trade but

Spinning Mill in Belper, England. This is the cotton mill where Samuel Slater was apprenticed before setting off for America.

who had been experimenting with Arkwright-type machines. It was the same year that Moses Brown and his son-in-law, William Almy, decided to start their own cotton textile factory.

Purchasing all the early American spinning-wheels, jennies and frames they could lay their hands on, they moved them into a rented timber-framed fulling mill on the banks of the Blackstone River, in Pawtucket, Rhode Island. The mill was surrounded by houses and it included its own company store. The spinning frames acquired by Moses Brown proved to be unreliable and unsuitable for factory operation, for the machines were too heavy to function by hand power and too faulty, troublesome, and imperfect to be water-powered.

It must be remembered that, in the early 1800s, the United States lacked the technology needed to compete with British manufacturers, and was dependent upon Great Britain for all their manufactured goods. With the end of the Revolutionary War, America had declared its independence, but was still dependent on England for its finished textiles. America also lacked the modern techniques of the British manufacturers. It was no coincidence that Moses Brown and William Almy, on learning that Slater had, for some years previously, held a responsible position as a textile mechanic expert under the auspices of Richard Arkwright back in Belper, England, sought his services. Slater condemned Moses' outdated cotton machines immediately. He agreed to prove himself by working without a contract for ten weeks while he constructed two new spinning frames sponsored by Moses Brown and William Almy. With his detailed knowledge, Sam set about his task, recalling all of his past experience to design and formalise his mill specifications. By 1790, he had actually constructed and installed two of the famous seventy-two-spindle machines in the Rhode Island Mill, all from memory (with a little help perhaps from sketches, plans, and even pieces of machinery he managed to smuggle out of England). The Rhode Island Mill was the first fully working cotton mill to be erected in America.

The Slater Mill, Pawtucket, USA. Designed by Samuel Slater, it bears a striking resemblance to the Belper Mill in England, with its almost identical cupola.

Although Arkwright's Spinning Frame, or 'Water Frame', as it was first known, had been invented years before Sam's arrival, this Englishman must have been delighted that he left Arkwright's workshops when he did – at the time, the British Government were fully committed to preventing patents from being used in other countries. For two years in the rented fulling mill with a staff of nine children, ranging from seven to twelve years old, Sam demonstrated the profitability of spinning raw cotton into yarn. At the end of 1792, Sam was made a partner with Brown and Almy, and they went from strength to strength until they dissolved the partnership in 1798, which allowed Sam to build his much larger mill, the White Mill. Ten years from the date Sam began his cotton mill apprenticeship back in England, Sam Slater used the Arkwright process to design and build a new three-storey masonry cotton mill on the banks of the Blackstone River, in Pawtucket, Rhode Island, expressly for the purpose of textile manufacture. Sam Slater even copied the English method of summoning the mill-workers to work by the early morning clanging of the traditional brass mill-bell.

In 1801, Sam designed and built a factory in Rohoboth, Mass., and, when Sam's brother John joined him from England in 1804, two years later, they established the manufacturing village of Slatersville, in Smithfield township, Rhode Island. Sam began the manufacture of woollen cloth in 1815–1816 at Oxford (now Webster), Mass., where he had previously built cotton mills in 1812. Later on he built iron foundries and more textile mills in Rhode Island and became a successful New England mill-owner. In all, Sam owned thirteen textile mills.

Samuel Slater is not only credited as the man who gave America their first successful water-powered spinning mill, but he will also be remembered in history as the man who first began the Industrial Revolution in the United States. Known as the 'Father of American Industry' Sam died in Webster, Mass., on 21 April 1835.

Today in Pawtucket, USA, Sam Slater's earliest mill, which he designed and built back in 1793, still stands as the Cotton Mill Museum – a testimony to the admiration shown to this very rare British emigrant

VIII

THE MISERIES OF CHILD LABOUR

Around 1788, from London and the South of England came the 'pauper children', to supply the evils of cheap labour for unscrupulous mill-owners in the North. The mill and factory workers, and even children under nine, were the ones who supplied the sweated labour and helped to build up the fortunes of the mill and factory owners of the cotton industry. Children of both sexes were employed, and six or seven was the permitted age for starting work (though it was known that children sometimes began work as early as three and four years of age). It was also sometimes the case that unemployed parents, whose pride made them refuse parish relief, were compelled by starvation to send their own flesh and blood to the cotton mills being built in the country where the streams and rivers abounded with water to provide free power to drive the machinery.

The machines required little skill to operate them, so an acute labour shortage was solved by using children. All a mill-owner was required to do was to enter into a contract for supplies of pauper children. Pauper children were classed as children dependent upon the Poor Law Guardians – these youngsters included boys and girls between the ages of seven and twenty-one.

This arrangement eased the burden of these societies, who were stretched to their limits with the financial worry of caring for them – they were only too pleased to rid themselves of the responsibility for those they were bound by law to apprentice out. Contracts for this scandal were to make up batches of fifty to 100 children to be sent off to the cotton mills for apprenticeship, and sometimes there was a stipulation included that, for every twenty children contracted, at least one mentally deficient child was included.

As the pauper children population was greater in the London and Southern Counties areas, this was ideal for the Northern mill-owners, who could now readily find cheap labour, costing them only the child's transport and their keep. The accommodation provided was often unhealthy, ill-kept, and paltry, lacking even the basic necessities of heat, light, and water. Many of the cotton masters considered the children as their property and gave them no more consideration than they would their factory machinery. Numerous orphans lived in fear, and suffered both physically and mentally through constant threats and beatings by the overlookers to keep them awake.

The Young Comfort Each Other. Their friend emerges fortunately unharmed(Illustration by Augustre Hervieu from Frances Trollop's book, *Michael Armstrong: Factory Boy*, published 1840)

The younger children were employed as 'scavengers' and would be sent under the machinery to pick up the loose and waste pieces of cotton, brush and sweep the floor, and mop up the superfluous oil while the wheels and gearing ground menacingly above their heads. This was an extremely dangerous practice, as they were expected to do their tasks while the machines were still working, often having to lie flat to avoid injury or death. These children were forced to crawl beneath the advancing mules and jennies to catch the broken threads then, with skill and dexterity, rejoin the broken threads again. Many children would become entangled in the machinery and died. They were paid 2d per day. If a child ran away it was common practice for the overseer to pursue the victim and drag them back to be severely punished, before being forced back to their mill shed. For bad behaviour, there was an instance, in one mill, of a boy being tied by his wrists and hung over the moving machinery; so close was he suspended the terrified boy had to raise his legs up high to avoid being badly injured.

Numerous children suffered from amputated fingers, hands, arms, and legs being caught up and crushed in the unprotected dangerous machinery. To ensure the mills were in full production for twenty-four hours a day, the children were made to work in shifts of at least twelve, and sometimes as much as fifteen hours or more per day or night. Those that survived to their adulthood suffered from permanent stooped shoulders and backs. Frequently, mill-owners manipulated the shifts so that, as one shift of children finished work, they could occupy the warm bed of straw of the next shift of half-asleep children being forced back into the mill.

To save money, the 'Prentice Houses' harboured both sexes together up to the age of twenty-one years, without supervision of any kind. This often resulted in corruption and depravity. Christian teaching was not forgotten, oh no, some pious mill-owners sent the apprentices to church on a Sunday, as long as they were not required for cleaning the machinery or sweeping the floors. Occasionally mill-owners were unscrupulous in their dealings with pauper children and, if their mill closed or was on short working time, they would pitch the children out of their accommodation and leave them on the roadside to fend for themselves, for the owners were entirely free from outside regulations or governing bodies. Derbyshire was no exception, and at one mill flogging of pauper children to keep them awake was reported. One girl threw herself into a millstream to commit suicide, but was rescued by an overseer of one of the more kindly mill-owners, who re-employed the child. Another unfortunate girl, of thirteen years of age, died in childbirth. Nearer home, there was the story of a sixteen-year-old boy who was employed in a Longdendale mill. The youngster objected to the mill-owner's instructions that all employees were to attend morning service every Sunday. The boy was ejected and the mill gates locked behind him. Undaunted, the spirited boy walked the 14 miles to Manchester, where he was apprenticed in a cotton mill. That same boy eventually rose to the position of assistant mill manager and later became a part-owner in a Scottish cotton mill near Galashiels, Scotland.

Regretfully, it was not until there was a severe fever outbreak at Radcliffe, Lancashire, in 1784, that the general public was alerted to the conditions of the pauper apprenticeships. Factory reform was painfully slow, but it was the cotton mills which first began to ring the alarm bells. It was some years later, in 1800, that Sir Robert Peel Snr, the father of the British Prime Minister, Sir Robert Peel Jnr who repealed the Corn Laws in 1846, was dismayed by what he learned from his friend and social reformer, Robert Owen, who admitted he was shocked when he first discovered the conditions of child labour in his own mills in New Lanark, Scotland.

Robert Owen believed that people were naturally good persons and became corrupted only after they had been treated harshly, and he constantly strived to understand the cruelties of poverty in the midst of abundance. Owen never employed children under the age of ten and was a strong opponent of physical punishment in schools and factories, which he would not tolerate

Padfield Township, c. late 1800s – Hadfield Mills (fronted by its mill reservior which still exists today). Part of the mill still proudly stands and is used for industrial purposes.

in his mill in New Lanark. Peel encouraged Owen to draft new regulations on the conditions for employing young people in cotton mills and factories. It was the British Government who made the first laws ever against child labour when Peel introduced the Health and Morals of Apprenticeships Act in 1802. The Act applied principally, though not exclusively, to apprentices in cotton mills and woollen mills, which included:

(a) Limiting the hours of work to twelve a day, forbidding night work.
(b) Boys and girls were to sleep in separate dormitories with not more than two to a bed.
(c) Compulsory education to be provided to all apprenticeships in the art of reading, writing and arithmetic.
(d) Every apprentice was to be supplied with two complete suits of clothing with suitable linen, stockings, hats, and shoes.
(e) On Sundays children were to be instructed in the principles of the Christian religion.
(f) Sanitation to be improved in all rooms and the factory had to be lime-washed twice a day and duly ventilated.

Local magistrates and clergymen, appointed by justices of the peace, were empowered to inspect the cotton mills and, if necessary, take the action to admonish offending mill-owners. Owen was disappointed that the new Bill had not gone far enough. When the Child Reform Bill proved totally ineffective, he realised that the Government inspectors were often friends of the mill proprietors, and bribes were often accepted not to report the offenders. In 1816, another Act was imposed, forbidding pauper children from becoming apprentices unless they lived within 40 miles of their parish, but this Act alone did not solve child labour and it took many other factors to improve conditions, one being the change from water power to steam power. Peel (Snr) continued to press for further reform and, with further advice from Robert Owen, the 1819 Factory Act became law, which was applied to cotton mills only, forbidding the employment of any child under the age of nine, with a maximum twelve-hour working day for children between nine and sixteen. All cotton mill-owners, including those outside the ever growing town of Manchester, were affected. It was, however, not until 1833 that a system of factory and mill inspections was successfully introduced to enforce the regulations.

In general, it may be said that mill-owners in rural areas of Lancashire, Longdendale, and Glossopdale treated their apprentices more kindly. Some had refused to take advantage of the Pauper Law Authorities who supplied the cheap labour orphans, although there was always the exception to the rule.

In 1851, within the seven townships of Glossop (comprising Padfield, Hadfield, Whitfield, Chunal, Dinting, Simondley, and Charlesworth), there were 3,562 children aged between five and fourteen. Of these, 931 were working in the cotton mills. One mill-owner, Edmund Potter, stated in 1856 that 2,073 children attended day school, and 556 joined evening classes. Sunday schools had accommodation for 5,150 children. It was not uncommon practice for mill-owners who had built, or contributed in building, the church of his faith within the neighbourhood to put pressure on their employees to attend their church. Non-attenders were duly noted, and on Monday morning would be firmly admonished by their cotton master for their lack of faith.

It is sad to relate that, apart from an uncommon few, many mill-owners were guilty in their day – driven by the greed for more wealth – to employ the evils of child labour.

IX

COTTON WORKERS OF THE
NORTH FIGHT BACK

1810. Beyond the mill gates, the dirty words 'Workers unite' were being whispered.

1811. Power-looms reduced the wages of the cotton workers, causing unrest and strikes within the cotton industry, and may have been the straw to break the camel's back. The Luddites rioted, mainly in the North and the Midlands from 1811 to 1814, burning factories and mills and smashing the machines which they had come to hate. It all began in early 1811, when the first of a series of threatening letters were sent to employers and mill-owners in Nottingham, from a supposed General Ludd and the Army of Redressers (hence the name 'Luddites'). The real Ludd is a mystery, and some believed 'the name Luddites was derived from Ned or Edward Ludd, who was deemed an insane or feeble-minded person who, through sheer clumsiness, destroyed stocking frames in 1779'. Whoever he was – General Ludd, Edward Ludd, or Ned Ludd – it was the name Ludd that spelled rebellion. And all were motivated by deplorable mill conditions and the use of non-apprenticed mill-hands.

Glossop also had a taste of rioting when, in early 1811, several spinners employed at Hurst Mill, built around 1800 (demolished 1938), and owned in 1811 by John and William Kershaw, brought charges against their mill-hands' illegal activities and rioting against their working conditions. Although they were sentenced to three months imprisonment, their later appeal was successfully upheld.

1812. The Lancashire Luddites were a militant group of hand-loom weavers who became completely disenchanted by the manner in which the mill-owners treated them. After numerous requests by the Luddites to the cotton masters for negotiations to discuss improved working conditions, eventually they were all rejected out of hand. In the early part of 1812, the Luddites became very active, smashing machinery and even stealing provisions without payment or without even giving a token payment.

Hosiers, cotton manufacturers and mill-owners could certainly be blamed for the conditions that their employees had to endure, but they could not be blamed for using machinery to ensure they were able to remain in business. Soon attacks on mills were taking place every night throughout the North and the offenders would often appear at a mill disguised, saying they had come in the name of General Ludd, claiming compensation, and placing fear into the mill-owners, who were horrified at the consequences. By now many of the cotton masters suffered from shot wounds and several were killed, prompting them to employ special constables armed with muskets. The situation was becoming out of hand and so, by mid-1812, Lord Liverpool introduced the Frame-Breakers Bill, making Luddite activities a capital offence. Prince Regent offered £50 reward to anyone 'giving information on any person wickedly breaking the frames'. On 20 March 1812, a warehouse was attacked in Stockport because the mill-owner was one of the first to use the power-loom in manufacturing cotton.

During April, the Luddites succeeded at their third attempt to burn down the steam-loom factory at West Houghton, Kent. The charge of arson resulted in four workers actually being hanged; seventeen more were transported to Australia to serve a seven-year sentence for similar attempts at machine sabotage. A serious attack happened in Yorkshire at the Rawfolds Mill on 11 April 1812, when the Luddites killed William Horsefall and mortally wounded two others. A total of 100 suspects were charged, sixty-four being indicted. A force of Manchester Luddites came by Tintwistle on 12 April 1812 and seized flour, meal, bacon and other provisions, and, although the shopkeepers sold them the goods at a fair price, the Luddites went down to Rhodes Mill, smashing machinery and windows and wreaking havoc, frightening many of the young mill-girls. Several of the men involved in the disturbance were later arrested and tried at Chester Assizes in the last week of May 1812. Three of them, James Crossland, John Heywood, and John Ellis, were sentenced to death, but were afterwards reprieved; other prisoners were sentenced to transportation to Botany Bay, Australia, for various terms, from life sentences to, in the case of the younger prisoners, seven years.

On 20 April 1812, thousands of Luddites attacked Burton Mill, Middleton, near Manchester, resulting in three of the Luddites in the crowd being killed by the musket fire of armed guards. In January 1813, at York, three Luddites were found guilty and were hanged on the spot, with fourteen others being transported immediately to Botany Bay, together with thirteen other men from Lancashire; eight of their compatriots were not as fortunate, and were executed. Other mills were assaulted in Huddersfield, Wakefield, and Leeds, and by now banishment to the colonies was the order of the day. If you were even suspected of being a Luddite, a Government clampdown ensured that you could be charged and, innocent or not, you could be convicted, imprisoned, sent to the colonies, or even hanged. By 1817, the fear of hanging subdued the Luddite fanatics, and they became no longer active. It is little wonder that many novelists spin yarns to create dramatic factory and cotton mill Luddite situations.

1812. The Luddite situation had caused a shortage of food in Lancashire and Derbyshire, with many poorer families bordering on acute starvation. This caused a Manchester woman named Hannah Smith to lead a group of mothers to seize potatoes for their starving families, solely intent upon feeding their children and the feeble elderly. They fled from the police, clutching their precious harvest as though it was manna from heaven. Hannah Smith, undaunted and alone, challenged the line of policemen, and with the bravery of Helen of Troy, rushed forward crying 'We will not be satisfied with only potatoes!' The policemen brushed past the vocal Hannah Smith, too intent on pursuing the escaping women. Quick as a flash, Hannah jumped onto an untended butter-cart and, turning to the startled onlookers, some of whom hid themselves in darkened shop doorways, she yelled 'Butter! You deserve butter', and, holding up pound packets of butter luxury, she cried: 'a fair price for this butter, a shillin' a pound!' Within minutes she had sold the entire cartload. She then slipped all her takings into the nosebag of the unconcerned feeding horse. Before she could escape, however, the police arrested her. Hannah Smith, in her attempts to fight bureaucracy for the good of the working class, was hanged at Strangeways Prison, Manchester.

1817. The summer of 1817 passed peacefully with a golden harvest and the mill business doing well. The Napoleonic War had come to a dramatic end in 1815, and it had cost the British Government £1 billion, leaving the country trailing in a state of economic depression – one of the worst periods in its entire history. As much as it had caused a rumble of discontentment throughout the land, it could not be blamed for what happened later on two occasions at St Peter's Field, Manchester. Long hours, low wages, oppressive heat, a mixture of foul smelling oil and raw cotton, together with animal conditions, had caused this resentment. Was it wrong for the workers to protest? Nothing wrong they thought, in presenting a petition to their respected Prince Regent of the North. So the weavers and spinners decided to march on London, to the seat of power and justice. Men and women began their march side by side, each carrying a blanket for the six nights of their walk to fend off the cold – the marchers became know as the 'Blanketeers'. They were well organised and well behaved and divided into groups of 100, each group having a 'Cotton Centurion' as leader. They invited the police to attend their meeting but the police refused, saying 'things never change, only time'.

The police were fearful of a rebellion against the civil authorities, for they doubted the good faith of the marchers. On 10 March, the marchers and their well-wishers gathered peacefully at their assembly point in St Peter's Fields amidst good humour and banter and hopes of a brighter future. The Blanketeers mustered, led by their leaders, three working class radicals, named John Johnson, John Bagguley and Samuel Drummond. The Dragoons promptly arrested John Johnson and the mood of the Blanketeers changed, filled full of hatred. Without warning, the Dragoons charged. The crowds scattered in disarray, and the Yeomanry followed in hot pursuit. In Stockport Road 160 men and women were arrested, the more fortunate escaped to Macclesfield and even Ashbourne, some only to find their path blocked across the bridges occupied by more aggressive Yeomen. They struggled and fought to escape their ferocious attackers. Twenty-nine men, including Bagguley and Drummond, were arrested. The worst violence had occurred in Stockport, where one man was shot dead and several Blanketeers received sabre wounds. Only one man reached London to present the petition to Lord Sidmouth, who promised to present it to the Prince Regent. To do what they did, the Blanketeers showed courage, yet conditions for the workers remained intolerable. A year later a cry went out to repel the unjust Corn Laws, an unwarranted tax on food. Two new leaders took up the struggle, Henry 'Orator' Hunt and Major Cartright, who addressed meetings in Derbyshire and Lancashire, and even as far north as Scotland. This fight back by the working classes for better working conditions would ultimately culminate in the bloodbath of Peterloo.

1818. The first organised strike erupts amongst the Lancashire spinners.

1819. On 14 August an orderly demonstration of thousands of men, women, and children once again marched on the doomed St Peter's Field, Manchester. The celebrated orator, Mr Henry Hunt, was making commonsense demands for political reform, with non-violence being the order of the day, but the air was heavy with tension and suspicion. Previously it had all happened, with disastrous results, and nobody wanted that again. However, the magistrates called out four squadrons of cavalry of the 15th Hussars (amounting to 600 men), a contingent of the Cheshire Yeomen Cavalry (400 men), a detachment of the Royal Artillery with two six-pounder guns ready for action, 120 of the Manchester and Salford Yeomanry, and all of the 400 Special

Constables of Manchester – totalling over 1,520 men of combat. The Establishment versus the People. The banners were high that bright early summer morning as the workers converged on St Peter's Field – men, women, and children, holding hands in unity. From Middleton, in orderly fashion, 6,000 people were led by Samuel Bamford; another 5,000 marchers arrived from Stockport. Only the aged and the infirm were allowed to carry sticks. The magistrates pondered: 'If an infirm man of sixty-five carries a walking stick, is that a weapon?' By midday the magistrates became worried by the crowd, now totaling around 50,000, in St Peter's Field. Fearing the military and the police were heavily outnumbered, the magistrates decided that this meeting – same as the last one – was illegal, and would be dealt with ruthlessly. The same magistrates could well have been mill-owners and factory lords. The Yeomen duly arrested the disciplined and much respected Mr Henry Hunt, and he succumbed peacefully. The protesters accepted the arrest of their leader, and, tightly packed together, it would have been unnatural if they had not buzzed in conversation. The Dragoon Cavalrymen rode high on their horses amidst the deafening, intimidating jingling from their equipment, and the distinct clobber of hooves. They advanced on the now 80,000-strong crowd, already suffering from dry, parched throats and nervous tension.

Confused, innocent people were desperate to escape from this unreal world, and all wanted to desert this field of St Peter's and return to the sanctuary of their homes. Then, without warning, the mounted Dragoons charged the commoners. Cavalrymen relished their orders as they split skulls with their gleaming swords, and the Yeomen, also with tightly held slashing steel, added further carnage to a flowing bloodbath. The grass from St Peter's Field that dreadful, pitiful day was stained with crimson, and littered with the dead, the maimed, and the wounded. Men clutching blood-stained banners. Women with hacked heads, revealed through gashed bonnets. Children recording everlasting nightmares. This gruesome day ended with eleven dead, 400 wounded, one in four of them cut down by the injustice of cold steel upon pulsing flesh and bone… 'And did those feet in ancient times walk upon England's green and fertile land, and did the Holy Lamb of God…' And it happened in the proud City of Manchester, once hemmed in by those tall, dark, satanic cotton mills.

Edward Baines, author of *The History of the Cotton Manufacture in Great Britain*, actually witnessed the Peterloo Massacre and, reporting in his father's newspaper, *The Leeds Mercury*, he blamed both the organisers of the event and the officers of the Yeomanry for the disaster.

At the trial of the organisers of the St Peter's Field Massacre, Henry Hunt was found guilty and was sentenced to Lichester Gaol for two and a half years; Joseph Johnson, Samuel Bamford, and Joseph Healy, were each sentenced to one year in Lincoln Prison. John Saxon and George Smith were both acquitted. While in prison, Henry Hunt wrote his memoirs, and explained why he had become a radical reformer. When he was released in October 1862, he again campaigned for adult suffrage and for Parliament reform. He constantly addressed the concerns of working-class people and campaigned for a ten-hour working day and an end to child labour. Henry Hunt was successfully elected as Member of Parliament for Preston. After his victory he led an estimated crowd of 16,000 people to Manchester and held a meeting at the site of the Peterloo Massacre.

1820s. After intensive negotiations between employers and workers unions, organised strikes by the unions were allowed, but workers were still faced by fierce resistance from their cotton masters.

1829. Another period of unrest throughout the North winged its way to Glossop when the spinners wanted their pay increased to 4s 2d per hour. On 18 December, the spinners targeted

Shepley's Mill, Glossop. It had started peacefully, with 3,000 mill-workers parading through the town, led by two brass bands gleefully playing, with people in a happy mood. Their mood changed when confronted by the locked mill gates barring their way to talks with the owners. The workers tried to gain entrance and came under fire from the mill guards' muskets, scattering the crowd back to their homes.

1830. Mill-owner John Wood was always known as a man of integrity, yet over at his Long Mill, in December of 1830, the spinners in the district had gone on strike for uniform payment. Rioting had taken place, resulting in a detachment of the Hussars and the Regiment of Foot Guards being returned to Glossop. Again the people of Glossop refused to give them billets.

During this time, the Great Eastern Weaving Shed, or the Long Mill, as it was by then commonly called, which belonged to John Wood, was being refurbished with machinery and so was not being used productively during the night. Because of this, the military commandeered the mill and decided to billet the soldiers on the third storey of the middle section of the building.

So concerned was John Wood that no attacks on his workers should take place, either by carelessness or deliberate provocation by the military, he slept at the mill whenever he was able during the soldiers' occupancy, taking a room where bales of cotton were stored.

Each morning when the engines started up, the noise of the revolving shafts annoyed the soldiers so much that their tempers flared. They were so agitated about it they deliberately set out to stop this annoying disturbance to their night's sleep by preventing the shafts from turning. One day, when productivity ended and the mill-hands had gone home, the soldiers tied one end of a rope to the shafts, and the other end of the rope to the metal ends of their beds. Next morning, woolly headed soldiers were surprised and shocked to find that, as the shafts began to noisily rotate as usual, the ropes coiled around the shafts and their beds were dragged towards the impending danger. The soldiers moved liked they never had in all their born days, and had to jump clear from their beds to prevent themselves from being injured. Much damage was done before the engines finally stopped. John Wood reported the incident to the military authorities, and for their reckless behaviour the troops were made to pay for the damage, money being stopped from their next pay parade to pay for the repair of the shafts.

1831. The mill-workers continued their fight for higher wages, but the authorities became more organised in stopping local resurgence. Coincidence perhaps, but, on 15 January, £400 worth of cotton was destroyed by fire at Glossop Railway Station. On 11 January, an unruly crowd of more than 300 mill-hands attacked Clough Mill. Mr John White JP ordered in the dreaded Hussars. A group of the attackers was arrested, including seven from Glossop and, when a troop of Hussars arrived in the town, accompanied by a company of Foot Guards, seeking billets for the night, Glossop folk, including all the innkeepers, again supported the fight for better working conditions by standing shoulder to shoulder and refusing such a blatant request. It was after midnight before the troops found accommodation in a cold and dark empty mill. The dejected mill-workers returned to work sixteen days later, still on their old pay. The mill-owners, including William Sidebottom, John Wood, and George Andrew, were jubilant – they had become richer – and to show their appreciation for the strong-arm tactics used by the presiding JPs, each of the magistrates were presented with an expensive piece of silver plate. Today, that would have been classed as prearranged bribery, but not, apparently, in Queen Victoria's reign.

1838. The Chartist Movement was formed and William Lovett drafted the 'People's Charter', laying down their aims:

1. Votes for all.
2. Equal electoral districts.
3. Abolition of the requirement that Members of Parliament be property owners.
4. Payment for MPs.
5. Annual General Elections with secret ballots. The petition of 1.28 million signatures was presented to Parliament but very quickly rejected, leaving the workers to fight on.

1839. In Glossop, on 18 January, due to declining business, forty-seven cotton masters of the district signed an agreement to work a four day week, the arrangement lasted for four months.

1841. The year of the economic depression, and individual misery within the cotton world. A second petition was presented by the Chartist Movement to Parliament, this time with 3,000,000 signatures, but again this was rejected, thus creating another strike by Lancashire mill-workers, but once again this failed. In August, cotton workers at Stalybridge came out on strike and organised a march through Ashton-under-Lyne and Hyde, recruiting more operatives as they wended their way to Manchester. On their return, and discovering that some of their fellow workers had continued to work on, the strikers forced their way into the mill and removed the plugs from the mill boilers, cutting off the steam power. This strike was never amicably settled, but was the beginning of 'nicking the plugs', and causing a disturbance in mill production. It made such an impact it earned the name of 'The Plug Plot'.

1842. The worst year to date. A year of unemployment, more unrest and wage reductions, more families experiencing food shortages, the mill-workers being influenced by the Chartist Movement – their only champions. For some it was 'employment on any terms, or else starvation', and for others it was 'stand up and be counted'. The 'Plug Plot' had spread throughout the North of England and, for a short period of time, there was not one cotton mill in Manchester in working order. A rally on Mottram Moor, with hundreds of workers in attendance, supported the call for 'a fair day's pay for a fair day's work'. Henceforth, mobs toured the Lancashire and Derbyshire area, forcibly removing boiler plugs to create a general strike. Again, Shepley's Brookfield Mill was targeted, as was Cooper's Holehouse Mill at Charlesworth, no doubt engineered by the Local Glossop Chartist branch as they indiscriminately broke into mills and removed the plugs. But old Shepley was prepared: his blunderbuss wounded four as he cried 'How dare they smash my mill'. Again the military were called in, only resulting in more bitterness to the Glossop working families, circulating as far as Hyde and Stockport. Famine and desperation drove the menfolk to again attack the mills. Shepley's Mill, in particular, became a target. The owner, Mr Shepley, barricaded himself in, guarded by Special Constables. The men started throwing stones and attempted to break the gates down in their attempt to enter the mill to commit further damage. Mr Shepley replied by firing on the rioters and eventually had to be escorted from his mill by a detachment of the 17th Hussars, but not before three of the demonstrators had been wounded by Shepley and a Special Constable had had two teeth knocked out. This attack was followed on 27 December by another, at Clough Mill in Little Hayfield, where they beat up the manager, resulting in the mill being closed.

The story of the men who were shot at by Mr Shepley was reported in the *Glossop Reporter* as follows:

On Wednesday last, the three persons who were wounded by Mr Shepley in the attack upon his mill at Dinting, near Glossop, on the 30th ult. were brought here from Manchester, in the custody of Mr Beswick, escorted by a detachment of the 11th Hussars, for examination before a magistrate, on the charge of riot, conspiracy, and of beginning the attack on the mill and premises of Mr Shepley, several witnesses were examined whose evidence established the fact that the mob attacked the mill, beat at the door, broke the windows, and that Mr Shepley and several of the Special Constables were repeatedly struck with stones and one of them had two of has teeth knocked out before Mr Shepley fired upon the mob. The prisoners were committed for trial at the next Chester Assizes for rioting and beginning to demolish the premises.

The peak of plug draining in the town was between 13 August and 14 September, when it was reputed that not one mill was working in Glossop, with many blaming it on workers from Stalybridge.

1850. The drubbing the mill-workers had experienced led to the decline of the Chartists. Demonstrators had died fighting for their cause, but extreme radicals had taken control, encouraging unnecessary violence. More importantly, a strong, tolerable Trade Union Movement had emerged and was gaining the confidence of workers. Many believe the collapse of the Chartist Movement was caused by the people's belief in democracy, with that unerring confidence in their elected Government, aided by that dubious sense of English optimism.

1851. An occupational census was taken on the number of workers employed in the various industries, which makes interesting reading. Although the cotton industry employed 527,000 workers, agriculture was still the largest industry, with domestic services numerically second. However, the cotton workers had replaced the building industry, and seventh on the list was the wool industry. At that period of time, not surprisingly, there were actually more people employed in domestic service than in the cotton and wool trade.

1853. With a revival in the cotton industry and an expanding trade in the Far East, the mill-owners were beginning to listen to trade unions, and the unions began to listen to the mill-owners. In particular, the Spinner's and Weavers Union changed their tactics, and promised the cotton masters that they would bargain more to win improved working conditions for their members, rather than their former strong-arm tactics.

1859. An analysis of the workforce in one mill employing 500 workers revealed that 50.2 per cent were adult women, 24.2 per cent were girls, 19 per cent were adult men, and 6.6 per cent were boys, thus revealing that three-quarters of the workforce were female. In this same mill, by comparison, the average men's wages was as low as 18s 6d per week, and women's 10s 2d per week. This was for a sixty-hour working week, in temperatures of 80°F, working in choking cotton dust percolating through the thick steam, with the unpleasant smell of thick engine oil causing nauseating conditions, and the thunderous incessant roar of the distracting machinery: nothing had changed. The cream of the cotton workers was the spinner, whose average wage could be 30s per week. The 'winders and warpers' regularly earned 25s per week, while the 'card stripper and grinder' could earn £1 per week.

One mill-owner, portraying an idyllic picture of conditions in his mill, boasted pompously: 'It is not uncommon to find in my mill the female workers overcoming the noise of the machinery by singing their favourite hymns.'

Hymns overcoming the noise of ear-splitting cotton machines or not, the wind of change was prevailing on the side of the cotton mill-workers of England.

Queen Cotton would have been delighted. The Northern cotton workers' relentless struggle against the mill-owners was at last bearing fruit, and in consequence, for a time at least, in the cotton towns of England there would be less children discontent, with hungry, bulging bellies.

X

MANCHESTER'S QUEST FOR WATER

Manchester's search for a new water supply to replenish their dwindling water stocks was accentuated by the rapid Industrial Revolution of the day, which caused a population explosion within Manchester. John La Trobe Bateman, eminent Victorian water engineer, gave his final recommendation as to where Manchester's new water supply would be situated, naming the beautiful Longdendale Valley, set in the heart of the Derbyshire Peaks. In his report, Bateman stated:

> Within ten or twelve miles of Manchester, there is this tract of mountain land abounding with springs of the purest quality. Its physical and geological features offer such peculiar facilities for the collection, storage and supply of water for the towns and plains below, that I am surprised they should so long have been overlooked. In the highest part of the Pennine chain, the river Etherow and its various mountain tributaries take their rise. Some of these form a romantic valley called – Longdendale. The water thus flowing from the surface and which may be collected in reservoirs will be as nearly pure as it comes from heaven.

Bateman's initial report never mentioned the cluster of cotton mills that had already spread themselves along the banks of the river Etherow from Woodhead to Vale House and far beyond. Longdendale and Glossopdale both had a domestic wool industry, dating back to as early as the fifteenth century, with small woollen mills, often built onto workingmen's cottages (some to supplement earnings from agriculture). By 1831, in the Longdendale Valley and Glossop areas, there were already at least ninety-two mills, fifty-six of them being in the Glossop area and a further thirty-six within Longdendale. The great change from agriculture to industry began as early as the 1700s, with the commencement of theconstruction of the cotton mills, and it is interesting to see why some of these changes took place.

The river water was harnessed by the mills and supplied them with the vital water power necessary to drive their machinery. Bateman had not mentioned that four of the mills – Tintwistle, Rhodeswood, Vale House, and Bottoms – as well as part of a Bleach Works at Crowden would be submerged beneath the intended chain of reservoirs. Another smaller mill at Torside (later a paper mill) would be severely restricted in its future development because of its close proximity to the proposed Torside Reservoir.

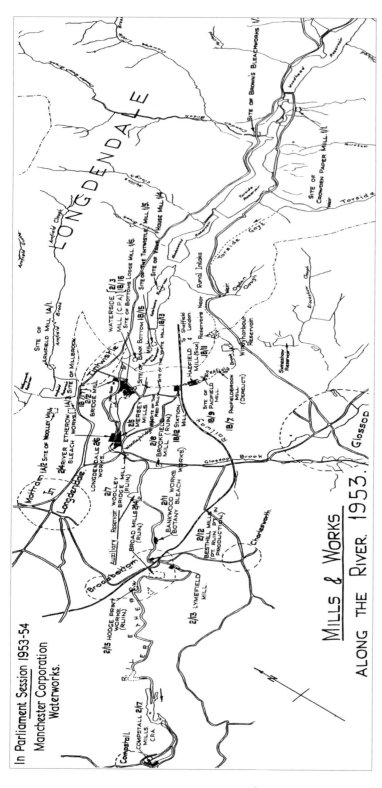

Map of mills and works along the river Etherow. This map was drawn up in 1953, to record and indicate the actual location of disused, derelict, demolished (including submerged) cotton mills, and sites of former mills alongside the banks of the river Etherow and Padfield Brook. MCWW was, at that time, seeking permission to reduce the amount of compensation water released into the river Etherow (during Parliamentary Session 1953–54).

Note: to locate each Longdendale mill photograph, match the reference number shown on the map with the reference number shown below each photograph (i.e. Bankwood Works, 2/11). This conveniently allows you to locate where the photograph was taken and its position on the above map. All photographs thus shown with a reference number were commissioned by Manchester Corporation during 1953.

56

Bottoms Gauge Basin. View of orifice sluices and chutes from the Test Basin looking upstream.
Waist-high handles over the pair of chutes operate traps to deflect water into the Basin when
checking the flow.

Understandably, the rich and powerful mill-owners, busily making their fortunes down the
line of the river Etherow, strenuously opposed Bateman's plans to construct reservoirs, which
at that time would not only be the longest chain of manmade water containers built one upon
the other on any river in the United Kingdom, but the largest chain of reservoirs in the world.
The mill-owners' concern was that holding water back to fill reservoirs would stop the supply
of water power to drive the profit-making machinery in their cotton mills.

From Bateman's report to the Manchester Waterworks, dated 14 October 1846, and bearing
in mind the mill-owners' opposition, he stated: 'The gross cost of the works, including the
purchase of water rights and compensation to mill-owners, to bring 20,000,000 gallons of water
to Manchester per day may be taken at £200,000.'

A year later, all the preliminaries of a Court of Inquiry had been observed and the Bill was
presented to Parliament on 9 July 1847, and duly received the Royal Assent. The mill-owners had,
by now, withdrawn their opposition, on the understanding that an application would be made to
Parliament, in the next session, for powers to construct further works and give the mill-owners a
larger guaranteed quantity of compensation water to be discharged back into the river Etherow.

The seven mills that had withdrawn their objections were: Vale House Mills, Tintwistle Mills,
Bottoms Lodge Mills, Waterside Mills, Best Hills Mills, Broadbottom Mills, and the Hodge Print
Works.

To this day the water authority, United Utilities, is obliged to pay into the river Etherow
10,000,000 gallons of water per day to compensate for the reservoirs being constructed across
the original riverbed and thus stopping the natural flow of River Etherow water, which had
previously supplied the mills with their water power without disruption. This water is still called
'compensation water' and it flows into the river, helping to keep it free from pollution.

Bottoms Gauge Basin. Plan view of the final Gauge Basin, showing river Etherow downstream from Bottoms Embankment, looking downstream towards Tintwistle. Remains of Bridge Mills in middle background.

The mill-owners also insisted that a compensation water gauge had to be constructed, in order that they, or their representative, together with a waterworks reservoir keeper, could each check at 6.30 a.m. every morning, and 4 p.m. every afternoon that the correct amount of water was flowing downstream towards their mills. The compensation gauge would be fitted, in the first instance, at Rhodeswood, upstream of the Vale House Mills, during the construction period of all the upper reservoirs. The gauge would then be removed to a permanent position downstream of Bottoms Reservoir Embankment on completion of the final works.

It was also agreed that the mill-owners would be entitled to be paid compensation for the loss of their mills, land, and property, including the mill contents, if these were to be submerged beneath the newly constructed reservoirs.

The river Etherow once flowed swiftly and silently down through the beautiful Longdendale Valley (meaning 'long valley') via Woodhead and Vale House, completely uninterrupted. The river Etherow still flows swiftly and silently through the Longdendale Valley, but it now flows via five reservoirs – Woodhead, Torside, Rhodeswood, Vale House, and Bottoms – and reappears at the foot of the Bottoms Reservoir Embankment before flowing downstream to the mills at Woolley Bridge. After swallowing the river Tame it flows merrily on its way as the river Mersey is born, and oh, what stories those two old rivers could share with each other as their gushing water journeyed from their source before flowing out to the wide, open, loquacious Irish Sea.

XI

THE LORDSHIPS OF BARON FITZALAN-HOWARD AND THE HISTORY OF GLOSSOP'S WATER SUPPLY

It would be an injustice to relate the history of Glossop's cotton mills without recalling the importance of water supply and other benefits enjoyed by the community through the good auspices of the Duke of Norfolk and many other mill-owners. They built many new mill cottages and, with surplus water from the cotton processing and fabric requirements, laid water supplies direct to the homes of the mill-workers to entice workers to be employed in their cotton mills and factories.

During this period a piped water supply was unusual, except in the homes of the wealthy, and the people of Longdendale and Glossop were required to carry water from their local wells, pumps, springs, and streams to their homes. In times of drought they had to rely on collected rainwater from wooden butts. As the history of the Glossop water supply played such an integral part in the building of the cotton mills, it has been included in our story.

The date of the original construction of the Goit is unknown, but it was sometime before 1794 when it was constructed primarily to supply water to the Duke's and other local mills. The Goit still exists today as a manmade earthen channel some 1m wide by approximately 1m deep. It is fed at its source from Torside Naze, Torside Grain, and Wildboar Grain, all feeding the Goit and flowing along an 800ft contour high up on the hillside, along the southerly side of the Longdendale Valley, on land owned at that time by the Howard family. It is capable of supplying 1,000,000 gallons of water per day, and is roughly 3½ miles long from source, feeding the Padfield Reservoirs before flowing into the Padfield Brook.

The courtesy title for the younger son of a Duke is Lord or Baron. The title Baron Howard of Glossop was created for the second son of Henry Charles Howard, the 13th Duke of Norfolk in the recorded Peerage of the United Kingdom in 1869. The 1st Baron Howard of Glossop was Edward George Fitzalan-Howard (1818–1883), and he was an MP and Vice Chamberlain to Queen Victoria. He was also the brother of the 14th Duke of Norfolk (1815–1860).

On moving to Glossop, the 1st Baron, or Lord Howard, as he was generally known, walked in his father's footsteps in promoting the family interests, taking them to new heights in the development of their mill business.

Coat of Arms – (Courtesy of His Grace, 18th Duke of Norfolk.) Records reveal that, on 12 June 1795, the 12th Duke of Norfolk Bernard Edward Howard (1765–1842), through his Howard estate office, indentured to lease the Torside Goit to Robert Thornley, who was also a new owner of the Vale House Mill. The lease survived from 1795 to 1890 and, during the latter part of this period, the lease was transferred to an Edward Platt, apparently as heir to Robert Thornley.

When living at Royle Hall, Glossop, together with his loyal agent, Mathew Ellison (1751–1834), they built further mills along the Glossop Brook and patently promoted the sale of certain parcels of his land to prospective interested mill-owners and businessmen who were desperate to construct their own mills on land containing a source of water power and sufficient area for workers cottages.

As there were 112 cotton mills throughout Derbyshire in 1831 (most of them within the Longdendale and Glossop area), it was fitting that a band of fifty gentlemen, to be known as the Glossop Commissioners, obtained an Act of Parliament in 1837 empowering them to construct three reservoirs for the use of the mill-owners. The reservoirs were to be situated on the Hurst Brook, the Chunal Brook, and Shelf Brook, but the fifty gentlemen were only able to raise enough money to finance Hurst Reservoir. As owner, the Duke stepped in and conveyed the land at Hurst to the Glossop Commissioners; the other two proposed reservoirs were abandoned. Thomas Ashworth was the engineer for the proposed reservoirs, and the surveyor was a young man named J.F. Bateman, who later designed and constructed the chain of five reservoirs in the Longdendale Valley.

The inception of Torside Goit begins here at Torside Clough. The Goit is diverted by the roughly constructed stone weir from the stream which then flows towards Torside Reservoir.

One of the first small reservoirs to be constructed by Lord Howard was Mossy Lea Reservoir, constructed in 1840. The Duke built this small reservoir to store water for his use, and for the use of other mill-owners. (See also page 70)

Three years later, in 1843, a consortium of mill-owners negotiated and agreed with the Duke for the lease of his land for the construction of Windy Harbour Reservoir or, as it was originally called, Mill Owners Reservoir, used for impounding water from Torside Clough, via the Padfield Brook and the river Etherow, for which the mill-owners paid an annual fee of £29.

Windy Harbour Reservoir was constructed jointly with Robert Thornley, to impound water from the Torside Goit. Although built mainly for the use of the cotton mills, some domestic properties also benefited, including the hamlets of Padfield, Hadfield, and the higher parts of Tintwistle. It was a smallish reservoir of five acres set on the hillside with earthen embankments. Recently, the reservoir was emptied and the earthen embankments dragged inwards and then levelled out and re-grassed, now almost hiding its original position. The springs from Windy Harbour reservoir still supply Blackshaw Farm.

General character of the Goit. Just an earthen channel lined in rough stone, yet so significant at the time for people and the mills. In some places it is covered by an arch of course-stone, covered with peat and heather.

Windy Harbour Reservoir, or Mill Owners Reservoir. The Padfield Brook originally rose about this point.

Padfield Reservoirs, Nos 1 and 2. Positioned one on either side of Padfield Main Road.

Railway Reservoir, Padfield, was a small reservoir of one acre with earthen embankments on all four sides. It was constructed by Lord Howard in 1861 for domestic consumption, water being fed from the Torside Goit.

Padfield Reservoir No.1 was a small reservoir of one and a half acres with earth embankments all round. It was constructed in 1863 by Lord Howard as a dual-purpose service reservoir, mainly for mill use, but also for domestic water supply to the villagers of Padfield and Hadfield, with water fed from Torside Clough. All surplus water then continued to augment Padfield Brook.

Padfield Reservoir No.2, was identical in size and construction to Padfield No.1. The reservoir was fed by water from Torside Goit, and used for the same purposes as No.1. Due to the ever increasing demand for more domestic water by the Hadfield Waterworks Co., the enterprising Lord Howard constructed Padfield No.2 in 1879. Lord Howard, always a benefactor, believed in supplying water to poor people who could never have afforded it otherwise. These reservoirs not only benefited the cotton masters, they also served the people of Hadfield and Padfield, who had the luxury of being served by a piped and wholesome supply of water.

In 1859, the editor of the *Glossop Recorder* suggested that Glossop needed a forum of local government rather than reliance on the gentry and mill-owners. Not surprisingly, it was the mill-owners, led by Francis Sumner, who objected to the suggestion, although the idea was supported by Lord Howard and Edmund Potter. It was concern regarding the water crisis between Lord Howard, Francis Sumner, and the mill-owners that finally led to the demands to press for a borough charter. The idea was again endorsed by Lord Howard.

Sumner and his crony mill-owning friends had opposed local government until now, but a Borough was different, for they saw themselves sitting in a council chamber with the prestige of being called councillors and aldermen, with the new powers that accompanied it. They too, therefore, sided with the idea of a borough council. The Sidebottoms of Waterside and Bridge Mills, together with many of the Padfield and Hadfield ratepayers, were bitterly opposed, yet their relatives, the powerful Wood family, remained neutral.

It was not until 19 October 1866 that the accolade of a Royal Charter was granted, combining the seven townships of Padfield, Hadfield, Whitfield, Chunal, Dinting, Simmondly, and Charlesworth to create the new Borough of Glossop. The actual new borough boundary was defined as all land and communities within a 2-mile radius of Glossop Town Hall, and it remains today a circle from the centre of Glossop, as shown on the Ordnance Survey maps. After the elections had taken place it was a certainty that the mill-owners would be elected by the direct ratepayers, the owners of factories and shops, and certainly supported by their employees, the mill-workers. Of those elected, eleven were mill-owners or cotton manufacturers. And who should be the first Mayor of Glossop? Of course, none other than Alderman Sumner JP. In 1881, Sumner was appointed High Sheriff of Derbyshire. He died in 1884.

The early pioneers of Glossop, who fought for a public water supply of piped drinking water, were the Whitfield Water Co. Formed in 1850, the company consisted of property owners in Freetown – twenty-four men and one woman. Their aim was to pipe water into homes from the Whitfield Wells, which had been built in 1849 by some of the company's founding members. Furthering the cause for domestic water supplies, Lord Howard, in 1854, devised a scheme, together with Mathew Ellison and his Howard estate office, to supply Glossop property owners with a piped water supply. To make a connection, the applicant was required to pay for the cost of labour, pipe work, and materials from the water main which he had previously laid down the High Street in Glossop. The recipients had to pay Lord Howard a water-fee of 2s 6d (12.5p) per week. The completed scheme resulted in the first water supply to Glossop. By now, Glossop was a fully fledged 'Mill Town'.

Although the construction work had provided new jobs for the unemployed, some mill-owners, fearing that the new water scheme was depriving them of precious water, protested about the legality of the new water supply. In 1864, Mr Francis Sumner, owner of the Wren Nest Mill, together with other mill-owners, threatened Lord Howard by an action of law. The man who had done so much for Glossop now found himself burdened with a large undertaking with little profit for what he had considered a public duty. Lord Howard promptly proclaimed that, from 19 September 1864, he would no longer supply water. A change was inevitable and, in 1865, the Glossop Water Act came into being, resulting in the formation of the Glossop Water Co. to manage the affairs of the four existing reservoirs. Not surprisingly, however, it was Lord Howard who became company chairman, and he was virtually left in control of the new undertaking who immediately concentrated their efforts on the four existing reservoirs. They converted the two existing Swineshaw Reservoirs into one, and increased their depth to boost water storage.

By 1866, the new Glossop Water Co. had completed the construction of Upper Swineshaw and Cote Lodge Reservoirs. To ensure a constant supply of water, the mill-owners insisted on Cote Lodge Reservoir being used as a compensation reservoir, for the purpose of storing water and releasing the water daily at a constant rate back into Swineshaw Clough. The amount of discharge was measured by a gauge on the side of the reservoir, 'for the Mayor for the time being of the Borough of Stockport or his representative' to check that the correct amount of water was being adequately discharged.

The 1st Baron Howard of Glossop, Lord Edward George Fitzalan-Howard, who had worked tirelessly to promote the cotton mills and domestic water supplies in the district of Glossop, died on 1 December 1883. He was succeeded by his son, Francis Edward, 2nd Baron Howard of Glossop.

Padfield Reservoirs Nos 1 and 2, Railway Reservoir, Windy Harbour Reservoir, Swineshaw Reservoir, and Mossy Lea, were all taken over by Glossop Corporation's Waterworks in 1929, but they lost control of the entire water undertaking in 1959 when, due to regrouping within the water industry, Manchester Corporation Waterworks became the new owners.

MCWW completed all new contracts then in progress and carried out further work at Hurst Reservoir, which was officially opened on 18 July 1961. Swineshaw, Hurst, and Mossy Lea Reservoirs are no longer in service.

XII

THE COTTON FAMINE AND THE AMERICAN CIVIL WAR 1862–1864

Calamity struck Glossop and Longdendale, and the whole of the cotton industry, in the shape of the American Civil War. It all began when, at 4.30 a.m. on 12 April 1861, the American Confederate Army fired fifty cannons upon Fort Sumter, at the entrance to the harbour of Charlestown, when South Carolina seceded from the Union in protest at Abraham Lincoln's declaration: 'Government cannot endure half slaves, half free...' Fort Sumter, after its capture by the Confederates, showed damage from the rebel bombardment of over 3,000 shells, ending in humiliation for the Yanks as the Confederates flew the rebel 'Stars and Bars'. Within five days, Virginia followed South Carolina and, within five weeks, Arkansas, Tennessee, and North Carolina joined them, thus forming an eleven-state Confederacy with a population of 9 million, including 4 million slaves.

So began the American Civil War. President Lincoln issued a Proclamation of Blockade against Southern ports, thus cutting off supplies into the Southern ports and stopping its exports of baled raw cotton to Britain and the rest of the world. The blockade was to last for the duration of the Civil War.

Many cotton plantations were destroyed by fire – either by enemy action, or by the plantation owners' patriotic act before fleeing their homes for safety. They would rather destroy their cotton fields than allow the enemy to benefit from all their hard endeavours.

The last cargoes of raw cotton, amounting to 170,000 bales, had been exported to these shores during 1860, and from then on very few cargoes managed to penetrate the North's shipping blockade. Once the stockpiled raw cotton had run out, there was an acute shortage, with the consequential closing of hundreds of mills, throwing thousands of mill-hands out of employment. Glossop was not famed for expensive runs of cotton and, as with many other mills throughout the land producing the cheaper cotton goods, mills here were hit badly. Within a year, 90 per cent of the Glossop mill-workers were put on short-time employment. With the closing down of the majority of cotton mills, 6,000 Glossop and Longdendale cotton workers became unemployed. In April 1862 *The Times* newspaper published a sad letter from a reader reflecting those hard times:

I look with a strange feeling upon the half famished creatures I see hourly before me. I cannot sit at home half an hour without having one or more coming to my door and asking me for bread to eat.

The writer had signed himself as 'a Lancashire Lad', but he could so easily have signed himself as 'a Derbyshire Lad', or even a 'Cheshire Lad', for the same conditions could have applied equally to the Glossopdale or Longdendale cotton mills. Queen Victoria was on the throne and, 'we have pigeons in our back yard and we feed them on Indian corn', so ran the song of the day, yet some working-class people were so desperate and starving that the only food they had to keep them alive was porridge made of Indian meal… but Queen Victoria was on the throne… Then came the middle cotton price rise of 5½d per pound, spelling more doom and gloom within the cotton industry.

More and more people had to rely upon the Guardians to stop whole families from starving. Henry Lees, of Woolley Bridge, installed cooking utensils and stoves for the use of his tenants and made gifts of food to them and others in the neighbourhood. Every Monday he gave out 2lb loaves of bread per family and one herring per person, on Wednesdays a pint of soup, and on Fridays a plate of potato pie. A Mr Jowett presented to the people of Chisworth 270 tons of coal, and 50 tons were gifted to the Relief Committee, to be distributed to the needy. It was decided that 2 cwt of coal would be given to the head of each family assisted, but the total cost to each family was not to exceed 2d. In Old Glossop, James Shepley gave 10lb of oatmeal to each of his employees, young and old alike. The Relief Committee set up a soup kitchen in Providence Hall and later brought more relief by advertising that, on Mondays and Thursdays, from 11.30 a.m. to 1 p.m., in addition to the free soup, they would sell hashed potatoes, costing 1d per quart.

In November 1862, two very large grants were made to the Glossop Relief Committee: £1,000 was received from the Manchester Central Relief Committee and £500 from the Mansion House Fund of the Lord Mayor of London. Light relief came in the form of a note from the subcommittee, whose task it was to investigate the applications for the supply of free clothing, informing the Guardians that: 'In going through the pawn-tickets of the applicants, we regret to find that females have pawned their underclothing and paying too much attention to their outer clothing, thus sacrificing their health and comfort.' No doubt the Eves concerned simply retorted 'Knickers!', or words to that effect.

During the harsh cold winter, commencing in December, the Relief Committee spent £7,380 on 4,678 people who were receiving assistance – this must have been the blackest period to date, compelling families to live on 2s 6d 'dole' money per week. People in abject poverty were held fast in the grip of authority, while the people in authority flatly refused to yield to concessions. But these people in authority were not of working class – how could they possibly understand mere starvation? They were the landed gentry, manufacturers, shopkeepers and prosperous tradesmen.

February 1863 witnessed the beginning of the most serious outbreak of discontent in Glossop during the whole period of the unexpected cotton panic. By now a large number of men were receiving relief money from the Board of Guardians, one of whom, amongst other mill-owners, was Samuel Shepley, who had been elected on to the board in 1834. The men had to undergo the 'labour means test' (testing a man to prove he was not working while claiming relief) – an edict detested by honest, God-fearing men. On 14 February 1863, a deputation was sent to the Board of Guardians to seek the abolition of this obnoxious labour test, but the appeal was flatly refused out of hand, without discussion. Infuriated by the shoddy treatment received, a meeting was called in Norfolk Square. The open air meeting resolved 'never to resume work at the labour test conditions, under any circumstances'.

The resolution that day is understandable, considering they had been ordered by the Board of Guardians to work for 'seven and a half hours per day for one shilling'. As those men did not turn up for work next day, the relieving officer refused to pay the large queue of men outside his office as much as a penny. The mood of the crowd grew ugly, not only because of the relieving officer's refusal to pay the wages due to them, but because of his demand for them to pay for the free food that had been sent to Glossop from North America. This was the Establishment sinking to the lowest level. The relieving officer locked up his office for the day and made a hasty retreat, only to be chased down Norfolk Street as he headed for the sanctuary of the Town Hall with the men baying at him and shouting 'Burrow up lads, the foxes are before'. The officer shot into the sanctuary of the Town Hall as the crowd outside booed and jeered and threatened before being dispersed by the local constabulary.

Bad memories are like ever growing shadows: as the evening rays of hope are dispelled, they fester and smoulder, never forgotten, rekindling as the early morning sunlight appears. Two and a half months later the festering turned into open conflagration when all able-bodied men were threatened with 'You don't do public work, you don't get paid, and you or your family will starve'. It is true that many of the more kindly mill-owners still gave food and sustenance to the families of their workers, not wanting to become involved with this aspect of the crusade of the Guardians, while other mill-owners gave the Guardians their verbal support.

The men had been uplifted to a lesser degree by Lord Howard finding them pick and shovel work constructing field drains and public works in Padfield and Glossop. The famine lasted until 1864, but during 1861 and 1863 the indefatigable Lord Howard found work for the unemployed by setting them to work in constructing small reservoirs. The unemployed built Railway Reservoir and Padfield No.1, between 1861 and 1863. The men were paid according to their skills, from 5s to 12s per week. Most of the workforce were mill-hands, mechanics, etc., unaccustomed to such hard, gruelling work. They had been half starved for two years, and the contempt this discontented, empty-stomached workforce had for the Guardians was evident.

The smouldering flared into a fire of hatred when, on 12 June 1863, picks and shovels were thrown aside and open insurrection turned into a riot when the men declined to work for less than 2d per hour. The men formed in procession and marched to the Boardroom at the workhouse but, as they were approaching, they were noticed by a member of staff, and the doors were immediately locked and barricaded. By then the men were determined to be heard face to face and, by brute force, they burst the door open and surged inside. The Guardians fled in terror. The police were alerted and six men were arrested and later bound over for threatening behaviour.

Official figures for Glossop alone showed that there was an increase of 300 per cent of paupers applying for relief compared to a year earlier, in 1861. These figures do not include some people who, 'even though foodless, were too proud to apply for relief'. Times may change, but the pride of many working-class people will never change. With all their meagre savings spent and all credit exhausted, the only professions prospering in Glossop during the distressing period of the cotton famine must have been the pawnshops and the undertakers. It was not only the cotton workers who felt the effects of the crisis – it was the entire town. Shopkeepers, clerks, tradesman, and warehousemen were all affected. In another survey, submitted in a return by a union official, H.B. Farnall, it was stated that: 'in twenty-seven officially distressed unions, Glossop was shown to have suffered the worst.'

From a purely statistical point of view, the proportion of the population in distress and applying for and receiving benefits in Glossop was 40.1 per cent, compared with 37.3 per cent in Ashton-under-Lyne, 29.9 per cent in Stockport, and 29.9 per cent in Manchester. Because Glossop was a smaller town, attracting little attention, focus was on the larger towns, and this put an even stronger burden on her resources. Many homes in Glossop and the surrounding area were destitute, and many families were left without a stick of furniture in their homes. Some families had to move into one house, sleeping on straw in winter and never taking off their clothes in an effort to keep warm. Little wonder that many were considering leaving their home town, with its previous happy memories, giving up their homes and emigrating to America, Australia, and the Colonies. By now, one half of the Glossop population were on Parish Relief and, if not for the sterling work of the Poor Law Guardians, who had the difficult task of handing out their relief funds, many in Glossop, Longdendale, and the villages around, could never have survived.

The Relief Committees were divided up into seven districts and, during this time, all unmarried mothers had to attend a sowing class for half of each working day, and school lessons in reading, writing, and arithmetic for the other half of the day. Youths between the ages of fifteen and twenty-one had to attend school five hours per day in the indoor market, with desks, forms and writing materials being provided by Lord Howard. Non-attendance at these classes could result in the loss of all relief.

The cold winter of 1863 was probably the one in which the greatest misery and distress was experienced during the cotton famine. A bitter complaint appeared in the *Ashton Reporter*, dated 12 December 1863, regarding the declared relief contributions when viewed in relation to the distressed families, which stated that, 'notwithstanding the colossal fortunes made in Liverpool by the cotton speculators, subscriptions to the relief funds from the Cotton Supply Association do not exceed £10 per annum'.

Prices advertised in the *Glossop Recorder* at that time for food (per lb) were: flour, 1s 4d; butter, from 7d to 11d; bacon from 3d to 6d; cheese, 7d; meal, 1s 1d per peck. Difficult for a family of six to survive on five bob a week.

Even though at the end of the cotton famine landlords had remitted over £20,000 to their tenants, over in nearby Stockport in 1864 over 2,000 houses became empty. At the same time in Glossop and Hadfield there were 686 empty houses, sixty-five empty shops, and fifteen empty beer houses. This exodus was partly due to families being evicted for not paying their rent (imagine their humiliation), and partly due to people leaving the district to seek work abroad. Waves of families began emigrating to America, Australia and the Colonies, relieved to be rid of Great Britain and all the misery they had left behind. The spring of 1864 witnessed a great wave of emigration from all the cotton areas, and so great was the result that a local newspaper was moved to comment:

> The swarm of migratory humanity surmounts every obstacle and spreads itself through the Northern States of America. There must be something peculiarly discouraging to our national life to cause the removal of such a large proportion of the population, and even those steering clear of the bastille in youth and vigour, unless relieved by an early death, have little prospect of old age, but that afforded by the workhouse.

Such was the commentary on the working-class conditions of over 140 years ago. Many specially constituted agencies stimulated the flow of emigration to the Dominions of Great Britain, by their desire to increase their population. This attracted more and more emigrant workers, and steamship companies cut their rates, until a steering passage to New York via Ellis Island could be booked for only £3 15s 8d. The Australian and New Zealand Governments went one better and offered absolutely free passages. By the end of August 1864, the Cotton District Emigration Society had organised the emigration of nearly 1,000 people. Over 200 people had left Glossopdale and Longdendale with new hope and the prospect of obtaining work and settling down in their adopted country overseas.

As Christmas approached, there was an expression of optimism and good wishes that appeared in the local newspapers: 'The cotton trade is not dead yet, it will live and thrive through all its disasters, and happy Christmas times will again return to Lancashire and Derbyshire. The members who have left and are now settled abroad will not return, but they will prosper in their new homes, and whether in Australia, America, or New Zealand, we wish them a Merry Christmas.'

In 1863, raw cotton began to trickle towards England. A total of 3,000 bales were landed in Liverpool, but none reached Glossop – Manchester swallowed it all. Although news of the raw cotton's arrival must have given the townsfolk new heart, it was only a slow dribble that begin to eke its way through. At first, only key operators were set to work at Henry Lees', Wood's, Buckley's, and Waterside Mills. An element of fraud by the Americans was discovered when some of the Manchester mills, on opening the bales, found stone packed in the centre of the bales.

Imagine the joy and jubilation when, in August 1864, the first large assignment of raw cotton arrived at Hadfield Railway Station from America – enough, it was calculated, to find employment for all operatives for four and a half days per week. Hamnett tells us the local paper reported: 'Good news in bad times. We have great pleasure in stating that the cotton mill belonging to Messrs Lee, Woolley Bridge, which had been closed for two years, has commenced work again.' As the first loads of cotton were transported by wagon to Henry Lees' Woolley Bridge Mills, the people went wild! Never doubt that a multitude of relieved cotton workers, together with their families, marched down Woolley Lane and Glossop Road and congregated merrily around the mill, waving flags to welcome the unloading of the cotton. With gay laughter and frivolous banter they came, simply expressing their total relief with faith and intense hope for a better future. They were so overjoyed that from their windows they hung Union Jacks and banners of all designs and colours, from a patchwork quilt to a richly designed Paisley shawl. Many a cotton worker's family would have celebrated over a pot of tea that day.

Later the Ashton Reporter heralded, 'a few days ago the first load of cotton for Woolley Bridge came to Hadfield station. A procession was formed and two old women rode on the bales of cotton, and a tea party was held to celebrate the event.' The cotton famine was about to end, but there were still many unemployed mill-workers. To help remedy the situation, between 1864-66 the Public Works Committee of the Glossop Union stepped in and paid for neccessary remedial work improvements to be carried out on Mossy Lea Reservoir. The recorded labour cost was £1,225-1s-8d; the total cost being £1,372-12s-0.

It was not until the end of the American Civil War, in 1864, that the employment situation began to improve. All wars leave scars, and the cotton industry was no exception. When the price of raw cotton increased, during the war period, from 6½d in 1860 to 27½d in 1864, there had been threats of more job cuts, but they rode the storm. For the present at least the future looked brighter, with no more families starving in such large numbers. During those hard times, fuelled by honest outbursts by the working class of a purely British nature, anger and frustration was at last beginning to be replaced by a feeling of pride, self help, and independence.

XIII

VALE HOUSE VILLAGE AND
MILL, TINTWISTLE

Quoting a paragraph from a thesis by an unknown writer we learn:

> In 1775, Samuel Oldknow, a native of Mellor, came to this district only nineteen years of age,
> seeking the best site for his first cotton mill. At Vale House he found it, a powerful stream
> running through a deep clough, and there the first cotton mill in the district was built – on
> the banks of the river Etherow.

Manchester Corporation Waterworks records confirm that the mill was constructed by Samuel
Oldknow in 1775 and that Vale House Mill, Tintwistle, was the earliest cotton spinning and
weaving mill to be constructed in the Longdendale Valley. It could thus truly lay claim to be
the first successful cotton mill to be built in the whole of the Longdendale and Glossop mills
complex. The mill was situated in line with Ashfield Gutter on the north side of the river
Etherow and about the midway point of Vale House Reservoir.

Manchester's Parliamentary Water Bill also revealed the following information: Vale House
was a village of 100 cottages with a population of over 600 people; the mill at that time
employed over 600 people, and many of the employees travelled from the nearby village of
Tintwistle.

The Vale House Mill boasted extensive premises with thirty-one rooms, two Carding Rooms,
nine Spinning Rooms, three Weaving Rooms, and two Blowing Rooms, operating fifty Carding
Engines, five Drawing Frames, 15,416 spindles and 326 power-looms. The mill was powered
originally by water and later by steam.

In the eighteenth century, Samuel Oldknow was synonymous with being a benefactor of
Marple, Cheshire. Mill-owner, road-builder, and philanthropist, he built the Mellor Orphanage
to accommodate child apprentices in his spinning and weaving sheds. Many of the children he
employed came from the Royal Military Asylum and spent, on average, eight and a half years
serving their time at one of his mills. On completion of their apprenticeship they were given
five sovereigns for having 'conducted themselves with fidelity and sobriety to the satisfaction of
their master' during their service.

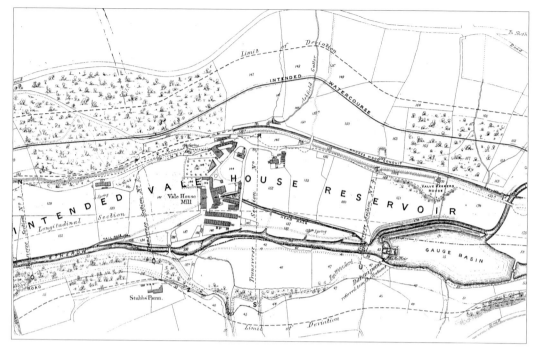

Parliamentary plan showing Vale House Mill and village, prepared by John la Trobe Bateman for the Manchester Corporation Bill (Parliamentary Session of 1853 1854), showing the proposed Vale House Reservoir (looking North).

In 1795, Samuel sold his Vale House complex to Robert Thornley and his brother John, but not before he began building his magnificent new mill near Stockport in 1790. Mellor Mill was a towering structure of some six storeys, 42ft high, and measuring 400ft long. The mill was originally water-powered, with a waterwheel named 'Wellington', measuring 22ft in diameter by 17ft 6in wide. At the peak of its production in 1804, the mill operated 10,080 spindles, employing a workforce of approximately 450 to 500 people, which included boy and girl apprentices, many of them former pauper children. Samuel Oldknow died in 1828, aged seventy-two.

Little information is available regarding the diameter of Vale House Waterwheel except that when the mill was first constructed there were two bevel wheels in the Water Wheel House of 4ft 8in diameter – the only power available to drive the mill machinery. We are aware, however, that the waterwheel complex was large enough for its machinery to have been covered by its own Wheel House. Vale House Waterwheel could well have been designed by John Smeaton, an early conventional waterwheel designer. From records and information of early cotton mill waterwheels, as an isolated guess only, Vale House waterwheel would be in the region of anything from 10ft to 15ft or more in diameter. The mill was fired by large twin boilers, supplying steam to drive a 40hp Beam Steam Engine which powered all the mill machinery. Steam also fed a continuous line of steam pipes to heat the premises. The condensing Beam Steam Engine had a flywheel, 24ft in diameter, with a 6ft 6in stroke. The circular steam boilers were 7ft in diameter, with two flues, 32ft 6in long, and were made by Fernehough and Sons, of Dukinfield.

The magnitude of the gasworks can be realised by the size of the gasworks equipment, comprising the following, which was sold during the sale of the mills: four gas retorts, 8ft long by 12in diameter, with a wrought-iron gasometer of 24ft in diameter. These statistics indicated just how productive gas heating and lights were in their heyday. The premises were extensive, consisting of: a Mechanics Workshop, a Cotton Mixing Room, two Blowing Rooms, fifty Carding Rooms, five Drawing Rooms, nine Spinning Rooms, one Roving Room, four Mule Rooms, four Winding Rooms, five Hand Rooms, five Warping Rooms, a Winding, Warping and Sizing Room, three Weaving Rooms, two Carding Rooms, four Self-Acting Rooms, a small Mule Room, a Throstle Room, and a Storeroom. The complex also included: two Weaving Sheds, a Warehouse, a Water Wheel Power House, an Engine House, a Boiler House, a Gas House, a block of business and clerical offices, and a Front Lodge and Back Lodge.

Vale House Mills next changed hands in 1834, to Mr Joseph Cheetam. By now the mill had become a very well-established Cotton Spinning and Weaving Mill – a great commercial enterprise, which led William Hobbs & Co. to purchase Vale House Mills in 1851. (The date 1851 is quoted from the Manchester Corporation Bill 1953-54, as also does Slater's Directory, which differ from Bagshaw's Directory of 1850, as stated below.)

The hamlet of Vale House appears to have been a self-reliant community in many aspects. Cottages had been specially built for the mill-workers, and a large house had been built for the mill manager. The village possessed its own shops and stores where the inhabitants could purchase food, drink, and haberdashery. Irrespective of Tintwistle's Church of England day school, Vale House enjoyed its own independent day school, which was built on the edge of the village. There is little doubt that the cottages and the school also enjoyed the advantage of a tapped supply of gas from the Vale House Mills Gasworks.

Bagshaw's Directory of Cheshire for 1850 verifies the population for Tintwistle in 1841 as 2,290 and records that 1 mile east of the Tintwistle Church is a cotton mill and a number of cottages on the banks of the river Etherow, named Vale House. Under principal residents, tradesman, etc., the following are listed:

(a) William Hobbs & Co. (company offices), Cotton Spinners and Weavers, Vale House Mills.
(b) Robert Slinn, resident manager, Vale House Mills.
(c) Potts and Armstrong, shopkeepers and corn and provision dealers.
(d) Lydia Gaunt, shopkeeper, Vale House.
(e) Joseph Roe, farmer, Vale House Farm.

From later sales of Vale House School equipment, it was estimated that the Vale House School could accommodate from twenty-four to thirty pupils. The pupils sat at their desks on wooden forms, and even had footstools and music stands provided, suggesting the children were being taught music; the schoolhouse even had its own small stage. It also indicated the schoolhouse was used by the villagers as a social centre, a reading room, and a village institute for other forms of recreation. All this activity would intimate that the mill-owners were benevolent people, believing that keeping their workforce occupied and happy meant a more contented mill with less disturbance in production.

It must have been a very unhappy day for many of the Vale House inhabitants when they learned their homes and livelihoods were to become a sad grave beneath a water-filled reservoir.

From a small booklet dealing with the Wesleyan Methodist religion in Glossopdale, written and published by a Mr Samuel Taylor of Tintwistle in the 1860s, the following observation was made regarding the Tintwistle Ebenezer Chapel:

Vale House Mills, before submersion. Looking in the direction of Rhodeswood Reservoir. (1/4)

The chapel was purposely sited at the east end of the village of Tintwistle, to be convenient to, and to cater for the religious needs of the inhabitants of Vale House, amounting to some 600 souls, who are almost exclusively of Methodist belief.

The chapel, built in 1830, still stands today on a hill between Vale House and Tintwistle and was affectionately referred to as 'Little Ebby of Tintwistle'. At least the inhabitants of Vale House would have taken consolation in the fact that their place of worship, high on a hill, was just that much nearer to heaven than the highest reservoir water level: their chapel could never be flooded by the intended plans in the name of divine progress.

When negotiations began in 1853 for the sale of Vale House Mills, between Manchester Corporation and the owners of the Vale House Mill (William Hobbs & Co.), Mr Charles Wilson, (1815–1874) was appointed as Manchester Corporation's representative. Although only brief entries, Mr Wilson chronicled in his diaries his meetings with the owners of the Vale House Mill. It is interesting to note that Charles Wilson cites Mr Hobbs and Mr Cheetam as owners, together with Mr Thomas Rhodes, and Mr Hobbs. Mr Thomas Rhodes was also the owner of Rhodes Mill (or Paradise Mill) and he was also the founder and owner of the Mersey Mills. Whether William Hobbs & Co. had appointed all these gentlemen to represent them, or whether they were principal directors of the company, is unclear. What is crystal clear from the entries is that Mr Cheetam resided in the Isle of Man. Mr Charles Wilson was a civil engineer and was initially appointed as the first outdoor superintendent of Longdendale Works, responsible for the large labour force and 'on site' engineering works. In 1862, he was appointed resident engineer at Longdendale Works, and served in this capacity for twenty-two years; he was responsible only to Mr J.F. Bateman and the Waterworks Committee.

As outdoor superintendent, Charles Wilson religiously recorded his waterworks activities in his diary each day, during the years 1853–1861. The diaries were discovered in the attic of Arnfield Tower, Tintwistle, amid the 1940 paper salvage drive of the Second World War. The 9 diaries were almost sent to Manchester for salvage! Willy Sharpe saw these as valuable records and confiscated them on behalf of MCWW. Willy kept the diaries and found them invaluable, using them as reference points during his research of the cotton mills on behalf of MCWW, before returning them to Bottoms office files, Tintwistle.

The following diary entries of Mr Charles Wilson, beginning 1856, are in reference to Vale House Mills only:

Saturday 16 August 1856
Travelling from Tintwistle to the Isle of Man with Mr Thomas Rhodes to see Mr Cheetam, owner of Vale House Mill.

Monday 18 August 1856
At the Isle of Man with Mr Thomas Rhodes.

Tuesday 19 August 1856
At the Isle of Man with Mr Thomas Rhodes. Mr Thomas Rhodes and myself were with Mr Cheetam, owner of Vale House property, all day today. [In the Expense Column on the right of the page it reads: 'Paid for Mr Cheetam's expense at the Isle of Man - 5/6p.' – an indication of where Mr Cheetam lived]

Wednesday 20 August 1856
Returning from the Isle of Man to Tintwistle.

Saturday 29th August 1856
Omitted 20th August 1856 – expense to the Isle of Man in connection with the purchase of Vale House – £5.4.0.

Tuesday 29 December 1857
Expenses – subscription to the Workpeople at Vale House who are out of work, per Rev. J.A. Page 5/-.

Saturday 28 April 1860
At Arnfield, Hollingworth, Torside, Rhodes Wood, and at Vale House Mills seeing Mr Tattersall (Manager) respecting Mr Hobb's letter to the Town Clerk about water being turned on for them occasionally to fill their boilers.

Monday 24 September 1860
At Torside, etc., at Manchester and back per railway.
At Bottoms Lodge Mill inspecting opening windows at end of mill opposite blowing room and putting additional skylights in Mill.

CATALOGUE

OF

STEAM ENGINE, BOILERS,

MILL GEARING, STEAM PIPES,

GASOMETER, RETORTS, AND PIPES, COMPLETE;

COTTON OPENER,

SINGLE BEATER BLOWING MACHINE,

With lap attached; Double Beater Ditto;

FIFTY SINGLE CARDING ENGINES,

36in on the wire;

TWO DRAWING FRAMES, TWO HEADS EACH;

Three Ditto, one head each; Double Grinding Machine; Five Single-Presser Roving Frames, 624 spindles, 10in lift; Seven Soft Bobbin Roving Frames, 640 spindles, 6in lift;

THREE PAIR SELF-ACTING MULES,

2,700 spindles, by *Parr, Curtis, and Madeley*;

One and a Half Pair Ditto, 1,112 spindles; Ten Pair Hand Mules, 6,480 spindles; Twenty-four Throstles, 3,464 spindles; Cop Winding Frame, 112 spindles; Cop and Bobbin Winding Frame, 284 spindles;

THREE TWELVE-YARD WARPING MILLS;

Two 9-8 Beam Warping Frame; One 8-8 Beam Warping Frame; Tape Sizing Machine; Sixty-seven 9-8 Power Looms; 259 7-8 Ditto;

TURNING LATHES; UPRIGHT DRILLING MACHINE;

Size Tubs, Spools, Bobbins, Driving Straps, and other Miscellaneous Property,

WHICH WILL BE

SOLD BY AUCTION,

BY MR. WILLIAM GRUNDY,

On WEDNESDAY, THURSDAY, and FRIDAY, 10th, 11th, and 12th August, 1864,

AT THE

VALE HOUSE MILLS, TINTWISTLE.

Sale to commence at Eleven o'clock in the Forenoon, each day.

May be viewed two days prior to the Sale, and Catalogues may be had from the Auctioneer, 86, King-street, Manchester.

MANCHESTER:
PRINTED BY A. IRELAND & CO., PALL MALL COURT.

Sale of Vale House Mill machinery – catalogue cover.

(Further extracts from Mr Charles Wilson's diaries, referring to various mills will be found throughout this book).

By 1864, Manchester Corporation had successfully concluded the purchase of the Vale House Mills, including all the contents and ancillary works, from the previous and last owners, William Hobbs & Co.

Once these negotiations had been concluded, Manchester Corporation wasted no time in selling off the Vale House Mills contents. From a catalogue entitled 'Sale of Steam Engine, Boilers, Mill Gearing, Steam pipes, etc.', the third day's sale, on Friday 12 August 1864, listed the following schoolhouse items:

501	Eight-day clock with two faces.
502	Deal cupboard, 4ft by 7ft 2in by 2ft 8in, with shelves.
503	Deal cupboard with box and shelves.
504	Deal desk, flattop, and footstool, two boards and colour pole.
505	Deal sloping desk, 11ft 6in by 2ft 9in on two supports.
506	Four sloping half desks, 9ft by 1ft 6in.
507	Three music stands and fourteen small forms.
508	Ten footstools and stage, 18ft by 12ft 6in.
509	Eleven wood forms, 10ft 11in each.
510	Deal forming entrance with door, 9ft by 7ft 6in.
511	20ft of gas pipe, 6ft of brass tube, ten bands, taps, and burners.

Sales of all the mill contents were held at Vale House Mills on consecutive days – Wednesday, Thursday, and Friday, the 10, 11, and 12 August 1864. The mill machinery included a Cotton Opener, one Single and one Double Beater Blowing Machine with lap attached, fifty Carding Engines, five Drawing Frames, two pairs of Hand Mules, nine Eight-Beam Warping Frames, three 12-yard Warping Mills, nine Power-Looms, twenty-four Throstle Spinning Frames, Roving Frames, three pairs of Self-Acting Mules with 2,700 spindles, over 1,000 various spindles, grinding machines, lathes, drilling machines, 20in saws, and numerous other tools and equipment. Also included were the Beam Engine, the boilers, and all the gasworks equipment. The merchants of Manchester and district must have invaded Tintwistle in their droves that week for such an important sale, and no doubt the Glossop, Tintwistle and Hollingworth Inns would all have been fully booked.

From the *Glossop Chronicle & Advertiser* (in around 1910) we read from 'A Local Man's Diary' by Joseph Thompson, a resident of Hadfield and a former employee at Vale House Mills: 'About 1869, the Manchester Corporation began to "drown" another place that is still a green memory for a few. My friend, the late Mr Samuel Taylor of Tintwistle said, "Vale House is a doomed village". And so it was. Shortly afterwards it was both doomed, and drowned.'

An account by Willy Sharpe, who was employed by Manchester Corporation Waterworks as assistant resident inspector at Bottoms office for many years, carried out much research on behalf of the waterworks on the district's cotton mills, and informs us of this revealing insight, dated 10 March 1964:

My Grandfather, John Sharpe (1834–1894), came from the Holme Valley, in Yorkshire, to work at Vale House Mills, along with his newly married wife, in 1854, but soon afterwards secured employment at his trade of Cotton Mill Carder, at the newly opened Bridge Mills, Tintwistle, built by the Sidebottom family, the newly built Bridge Mills commenced working in 1854. It is very probable that in the following years, many Vale House villagers followed his example and became employed at Bridge Mills or the neighbouring Waterside Mills, of the same Sidebottom family, which were then at the height of their success and employing between them at both mills some 6,000 to 7,000 workpeople. It occurs to me that from 1854, onwards, the gradual evacuation of the village of Vale House began, when the villagers began moving to Tintwistle and Hadfield for employment in larger and possibly more modern mills. As a small concern the employees of Vale House Mills would be the first to be affected by trade recession, and in particular the falling off in the cotton trade which followed on during and after the Crimean War of the 1850s.

The comment referring to the trade recession is supported by Mr Wilson's diary entry of 29 December 1857 regarding the 'Workpeople of Vale House who are out of work'.

Apart from trade recessions there would also be the foreshadowing of the waterworks, requiring Vale House as another reservoir, the idea of which was beginning to take shape in the latter part of the 1850s. It is therefore possible to assume that, by 1865, there would be but few people left in Vale House Village. For parish purposes Vale House would be included in the village of Tintwistle population which, in the census of 1861, was about 3,800 persons. There would thus be no wholesale mass evacuation of the hamlet as the villagers, realising they were living there for a limited period only, would have made their plans accordingly, and moved as opportunity occurred to new dwellings and occupations in Tintwistle, Hadfield, and the neighbourhood.

General view of the Hadfield Mills complex in its heyday.

There is little doubt that there was no mass exodus from Vale House. The slow abandonment of the village had indeed begun in the late 1860s, with the realisation that Vale House would be included in the chain of reservoirs as part of a proposed new water supply for Manchester. It would begin as a slow trickle at first and would gain momentum in about 1857, when unemployment was beginning to bite. The farewells would be further increased when news reached them of a new mill being built at Bridge Mill, Hollingworth. But it must be remembered that many of the older villagers will have been deeply saddened at having to leave the place where most of their younger memories had been kindled, and in the future would have to be relived beneath a barrier of cold water. To the younger villagers especially, the impulse to run for survival must have been of paramount importance, encouraged by the possibility of working in a modern mill, with the added incentive of new cottages being available to the mill-workers. Better to go than wait to be drowned.

The photograph (1/4) shows the Vale House Mills chimney, which protruded from the water of the reservoir for some years and was not demolished until 1887, at the request of the Manchester to Sheffield Railway Co. They feared for the stability of the moving train, which could overturn if passengers crowded over to the reservoir side of the train to catch a glimpse of the phenomenon of a stone mill chimney protruding from a sheet of still cool water.

Extracts from original handwritten reports of John la Trobe Bateman, consulting engineer, sent to the Manchester Corporation Waterworks Committee regarding Vale House Mills gives further historic reading. Some Waterworks Committee reports, as shown below, were signed by Mr Charles Wilson, who by this time had been promoted to resident engineer at Longdendale Works:

Vale House chimney. (1/4)

29 October 1863 – Works subcommittee.

I beg to report that the various works have been progressing. It appears that during the time the Vale House Mills have been untenanted the following persons have been employed, viz.

Thomas Whittington, Bookbinder, at 8/- per week.

James Forrester, Overlooker, at 7/6d per week.

John Bowden, Fireman, at 5/- per week.

Sarah Ripley, Housekeeper, at 7/- per week.

Arrangements have been made to continue their services for the present. It appears that during the summer it has taken about 3 or 4 tons of coal per week to warm the rooms, but this quantity may have to be increased if the machinery remains in the mill during the winter. With reference to the purchase of Armfield Mill, it appears to me very desirable for the Corporation to purchase the property in readiness for their future Arnfield Reservoir.

5 July 1864 – Town Hall, Manchester.

Amongst these works is the road from Tintwistle to Vale House Mills, on which the men could be immediately set to work and proceeded with as rapidly as possible for the purpose of facilitating the delivery of stone and other materials which may have to be brought in from a distance. [These reports demonstrate that, once the Parliamentary powers had been sanctioned, Mr Wilson was eager to commence work on Vale House Reservoir.]

7 July 1864 – Town Hall, Manchester

Gentlemen, I beg to report (as instructed), on the particulars connected with the machinery at Vale House with reference to its sale. Two questions appear to require considering,

(1) Is it desirable to sell the machinery at all?

(2) If it be desirable to sell it, is it desirable to sell it now?

With reference to the first question, I believe it is desirable to sell the machinery because firstly, if the proposed reservoir at Rhodes Mill be constructed then in that case Vale House Mills will be destroyed, and secondly, should the proposed reservoir not be constructed but a tenant found for Vale House, the machinery is of a character which cannot again be profitably worked. With reference to the second question, it is very doubtful if anything will be gained by deferring the sale of the machinery. It is very probable that whenever it is sold it will have to be sold as old metal and it is not likely that by keeping it say another year (or any longer time) that there will be such an increase in the price of old metal as will be the equivalent to the expenses (viz. upwards of £200 per year) which are being incurred for the cost of wages and rates. I am Gentlemen, your obedient servant, Charles Wilson. [Sale of above machinery, see pages 76-77.]

7 July 1864

I beg to report that in repairing and laying pipes the trenches have frequently to be kept open during the night and it has hitherto been the custom for the watchman to have fires in open grates, placed near such open trenches for the protection of the public. Attention has been drawn to the dangerous character of these open grates and to the probability which there is that (especially during high winds) sparks may be blown from them into buildings or other premises (at the vacated and empty Vale House Mills) and cause serious fires, and it has been suggested that instead of fires we should use lamps like that used for similar purposes by the Highway Department. In consequence of this suggestion we have tried lamps which we have borrowed from Mr Kelly and they appear to answer well, and I beg to suggest that we use lamps instead of grates whenever practical in future. We shall still be obliged to have grates in fires to melt lead etc., but these may not be kept-in, for the purpose of watching the open trench.

16 November 1865

A deputation from the farmers in Tintwistle visited me yesterday morning for the purpose of ascertaining whether the Corporation would allow them to have use of the empty premises at Vale House to use as a hospital in the event of the Cattle Plague visiting the district. I told them that I would lay the matter before you and inform them of your decision.

23 November 1865

I am sorry to have to report that a man named Charles Scott was injured by a large stone falling on his head when at the bottom of the trench at Vale House and although surgical aid was immediately obtained and everything was done for him that could be done died on the 27th ult. I understand he left four little children unprovided for.

Thus the final execution of the largest and most employed mill in the Longdendale Valley at that time was signed and sealed. Construction of the Vale House Reservoir was completed in July 1869, and the people who had lived there all their lives must have been saddened to see their street, their house, their shops, and the old schoolhouse being slowly drowned, day by day, as the water kept on rising.

There was nothing they could do about it, except call upon fond memories of their happy hamlet. Yet Vale House Cotton Mill had the last laugh for, when the reservoir is extremely low, the weir, goit, and the remains of the stone mill buildings are still visible, to remind us of a drowned village of long ago.

XIV

THE HISTORY OF THE MILLS
AND WORKS OF GLOSSOPDALE
AND LONGDENDALE

Fulling mills caused a minor 'industrial revolution' during the last half of the twelfth century, when the earliest fulling mills were introduced into England by the Cistercian Monks and Knights Templars. Fulling mills were used to process the cloth made from wool. After a piece of woollen cloth had been woven, the fibres of its fabric were loose, airy, and unmeshed, similar in appearance and texture to a piece of cheese cloth. To make the woollen material more comfortable to wear, it was put through a process of 'fulling', which literally thumped or pounded the cloth repeatedly with large wooden hammers in pits filled with a mixture of water, urine, and fullers-earth. Once the fulling had been completed and the fats and other impurities had been removed, the cloth was rinsed, before being stretched out on racks to dry. The cloth was finally rolled and bundled to complete the process.

From a map of 1767, one could claim that Waterside, Hadfield, was the site of the earliest fulling mill built in Glossopdale and Longdendale, with a further fulling mill being built at the bottom of Littlemoor in 1781.

Old Paper Mill, Crowden

As for the construction of mills in the Longdendale Valley, the first mill to be mentioned in the Parliamentary Act of 1847 was Old Paper Mill. In Kelly's Directory of Derbyshire for 1848 and 1849, the owner is listed as 'Thomas Turner, Paper Maker, Torside'. Constructed before 1847, and situated about 500 yards south-west of the old Crowden Railway Station, and on Fair Vage Clough, the mill was a small two-storey factory with a dwelling house in the same block. It first produced cotton cord, before being converted by Thomas Turner of Torside into a paper mill. A mill pond or mill lodge was shown on earlier plans, which included a waterwheel. From Willy Sharpe, the assistant resident inspector, who interviewed an ex-waterworks workman in 1960, we learn:

> Earnest Povey stated that he lived in the Paper Mill's Cottage during 1914–1916. He had just returned from Canada and the then Resident Inspector, Mr Fairbrother, offered Povey a job as Assistant Reservoir Keeper at Woodhead, with accommodation at Paper Mill's Cottage on a rental of two shillings and sixpence per week. Povey objected to paying rent so Mr Fairbrother,

who was desperate for someone to take on the job in the wild conditions of winter at Woodhead agreed to pay Povey an extra halfpenny an hour based on a working fifty-six-hour week, Povey accepted, and commenced work on 23 March 1914. During his time living there, Povey said that the Railway Company was undergoing rail track widening. The contractors horses were stabled in the lower part of paper mill, with stalls being made especially for them; provender was stored in the upper part of the mill. Povey lived at the Paper Mill Cottage for two years prior to joining the Army in the First World War. On being demobbed he started his own business as a coal dealer in Tintwistle, where he resided until his death in the late 1960s.

Two other assistant keepers followed Povey to the cottage. Walter Miller, was tenant for two years, then replaced by John W. Goddard, who stayed there until 1920, prior to moving to a house at Stone Row, Crowden. Goddard was the last person to live in Paper Mill Cottage.

Extract from Mr Charles Wilson's diary, as shown below, refers to Crowden Paper Mill:

23 March 1859
Return by 11.30. train with Mr Urquhart and take him to the Paper Mill, Woodhead, for Turners to complete conveyance of Paper Mill to Manchester Corporation.

Although in a very dilapidated condition, the Crowden Mill ruins were clearly still visible until the year 2000, when it was sold by North West Water to a private buyer, who converted it into a desirable residence which bears little resemblance to the Paper Mill of long ago.

Crodden Mill, of which little is known, except that it was presumably built before 1834, was situated near Crowden. On the Parliamentary plan of 1836, Crodden Mill was situated on the south of the river Etherow, between Torside Brook and Wildboar Clough. It was reputed to have been a cotton spinning and manufacture owned by Hadfield & Wilkinson, but the owners could never be traced.

I remember in 1965 seeing the foundation stones of the nearby historic Crowden Hall, which were barely visible at the time. Since then they have disappeared without trace. Crowden Hall was built by the Hadfield family in 1692, and they were regarded as the local squires of the Crowden area. The builder's great grandson (1756–1803) was hanged in Carlisle in 1803; he was the protagonist in the well-written novel by Melvyn Bragg, *The Maid of Buttermere*.

Brown's Bleach Works, Crowden

A small country works, situated on the north side of Torside Reservoir, just on the east of Crowden Brook, where it enters the reservoir. It was constructed before 1846 by Thomas & William Brown, bleachers. The main building was L-shaped, measuring about 20 yards by 12 yards. It also had other sheds, stables, and the usual gasometer, etc. There were two lodges, and a waterwheel, powered by water fed from a goit from 'Brown's Spring'. Manchester Waterworks Committee purchased the complex in 1867 and maintained it through the years, using it for storage. Of late the buildings have been badly vandalised, with most of the roof slates removed. Demolition, or sale to a private buyer for development, is its probable future. The outline of the lodges and certain watercourses are still traceable on the ground. Most of the buildings have since disappeared, but the cart shed and joiner's shop, known as 'Mill Yard', still remain. It possessed two residences nearby, named 'Stone Villas', which still remain today, and are regularly maintained by the owners, United Utilities, through the years. The villas have been constantly occupied by reliable and dependable tenants.

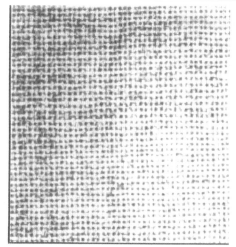

View of the weave of cloth, immediately after it has been removed from the loom, showing the open nature of the fabric.

The same piece of cloth after it has been fulled. The yarns have now closed up and become more compact and even.

Above: Contrast of cloth before and after fulling.

Left: Seventeenth-century fulling mill.

Opposite above: Old Paper Mill, Crowden (formally Kidfield Mill), overlooking Torside Reservoir on south side of valley. (1/1)

Opposite below: Brown's Bleach Works, Crowden, looking south-west. (1/3)

Tintwistle Mill, later Rhodes Mill (or Paradise Mill)

Situated at Bottoms Reservoir, opposite the quarry, from which much of the quarry stone was dressed for the magnificent stonework construction of the reservoirs. The mill was built in 1777 by Thomas Thornley of Padfield, who sold it to Thomas Rhodes & Sons, of Tintwistle, in 1834, who immediately changed the mill's name to Rhodes Mill. In 1857, Thomas Rhodes went into partnership, and the firm became Rhodes & Armstrong. The mill became known as Paradise Mill. The mill was much smaller than the Vale House Mills. It was taken over by Manchester Corporation and remained unoccupied from 1864, before being submerged in Bottoms Reservoir 100 years after it had been built. We know more about Thomas Rhodes than the mill he owned, for he built Mersey Mills in 1859, followed by the Hadfield Mill in 1873. He was a member of the first elected Glossop Borough Council, representing Hadfield, and was eventually made an alderman, and later the Mayor of Glossop. He built his residence, Mersey Bank House, in 1862. On his death in 1883, his three sons inherited the mills: George Wood Rhodes inherited the Mersey Mill Co., and William Shipley Rhodes and Herbert Rhodes, the latter noted as a great amateur cricketer, took control of Padfield Mill.

Bottom Lodge Mill, Tintwistle

Built in 1795 by John Turner. The business was continued by his son William until owned by John Winterbottom in 1834, who was a cotton spinner from Tintwistle. The mill was in the vicinity of Tintwistle Mill at Bottoms. It was smaller than Vale House Mill but, with fairly extensive premises, it was greater than Rhodes Mill, housing twenty-one Carding Rooms, five Spinning Rooms, and four Weaving Sheds. Power was provided via its goit to a waterwheel measuring 22ft in diameter and 16ft 16in wide. It possessed a steam boiler, 26ft in length and 8ft in diameter, providing power to drive a 130hp steam engine and a 1,105hp waterwheel. The mill changed hands in 1851, with John's son, John Winterbottom Jnr, taking over. Slater's Directory for 1855 names the owner as Bottoms Lodge Mill Co. before it was bought by Manchester Corporation Waterworks Committee in 1954–5. They immediately leased it to Robert Cross & Co., cotton spinners, of Tintwistle. It is recorded that the rent charged from 25 March to 14 May 1858 was £130. The mill was submerged in Bottoms Reservoir (see photograph, page 88).

Arnfield Mill, Tintwistle

Situated about ½ mile north-north-west of Tintwistle on the Arnfield Brook, this was a small country factory of 0.31 acres, and had a goit, lodges, gasometer, etc. It was built by William Buckley in 1828 for cotton spinning and manufacturing. It changed hands in 1834, when bought by John Robert Hull of Arnfield Hall, in 1834. Bagshaw's Directory of Cheshire, 1850, reads:

> Armfield is a small hamlet, three-quarter miles north of Church at Tintwistle, here calico printing was formerly carried out, but the premises are now unoccupied.

In 1874, when MCWW submerged the hamlet of Armfield beneath their reservoir, MCWW also named their reservoir Armfield Reservoir (as named on the Ordnance Map.) Somewhere along the way the reservoir was renamed, Arnfield. It is worth noting that all of Bateman's reports to his committee were hand written which might account for the name change. By 1954, the mill had been completely demolished. Little else is known.

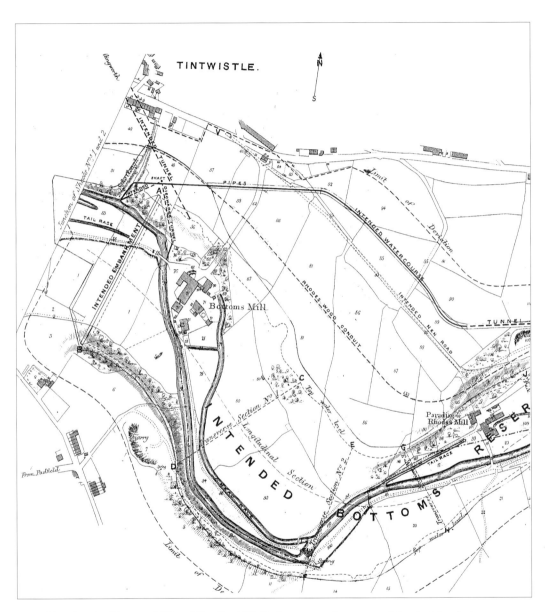

Plan showing Bottoms Mill and Paradise Mill. Parliamentary plan, prepared for the Manchester Corporation Bill (Parliamentary Session 1853–1865), showing the intended Bottoms Reservoir.

Bottom's Lodge Mill, Tintwistle, 1860. A blend of rural tranquility – agriculture and industry.

A Manchester Waterworks Committee report, dated 1867, reads: 'The Committee have purchased the premises called Armfield Mill, situated at the Armfield Reservoir, and are arranging for the purchase of the Bleach works at Crowden Brook, at the head of Torside Reservoir. After these Bleach works are purchased, the Torside Reservoir may be filled to top level, without further compensation, and then no manufacturing process will be carried on upon the drainage or gathering ground of the Corporation's.' From a catalogue of sale held at Bottoms Lodge Mills, Tintwistle, on Wednesday 16 October 1867, we glean further knowledge regarding the layout of the mill: Spinning Room, store room, offices, one Card Room, three Spinning Rooms, Roving and Bobbin Room, Roller Converting Room, five Spinning Rooms. Also listed, under New Mill: ten Weaving Rooms, Engine House, Waterwheel House and Smithy with fodder room over it.

Woolley Mill

Built before 1840 as a woollen mill, beside Arnfield Brook, two thirds of a mile from Tintwistle. By 1864, it was owned by William & John Robert as a gutta-percha factory. The mill manufactured cotton banding, gutta-percha cylinders, and printer's bowls for calico printing. Kelly's Directory for 1851, 1855, and 1865, gives the owner as Michael Joseph Dalton (possibly a relative of Thomas and John Dalton at Hollingworth Print Works). The mill had a goit and reservoirs and probably a waterwheel. Completely demolished by 1953 (see photograph, page 90).

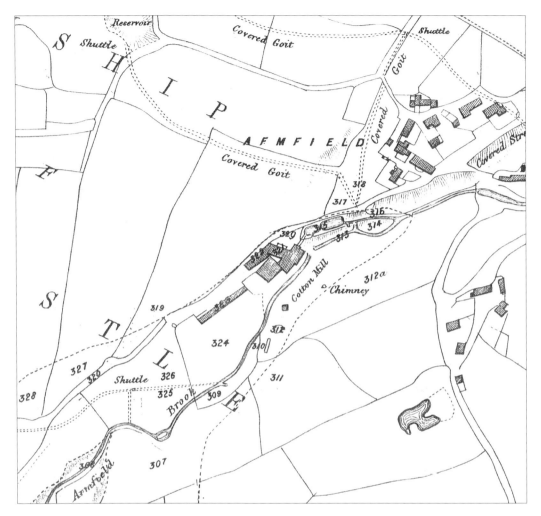

Ordnance Map dated 1846, showing Armfield Mill and the hamlet of Armfield. Demolished during the construction of Arnfield Reservoir.

Millbrook Mill (later Millbrook House)

Partly in Hollingworth and Tintwistle, astride the Hollingworth Brook on the Manchester to Sheffield Road. The mill was built east of Tintwistle, and was a very well built stone factory of moderate size (area of 0.54 acres), including goit lodges and waterwheel. This mill was solely owned by the Sidebottom family (another famous local name). Brothers William and George Sidebottom built the mill in 1790. When William died in 1834, the mill was shared between George and his nephew, Ralph Sidebottom. On the death of Uncle George by 1843, Ralph became sole owner and ran the mill for the next twenty years. In 1831, six men were committed to Chester Assizes for outrage at Millbrook Mill; a detachment of the 10th Hussars escorted them to Ashton-under-Lyne. Ralph died in 1863 and, by 1865, his son Ralph had been named executor of Millbrook Mill and estate. Ralph decided it was time to retire, so he simply ceased business and converted the mill into the existing large, imposing residence known as Millbrook House.

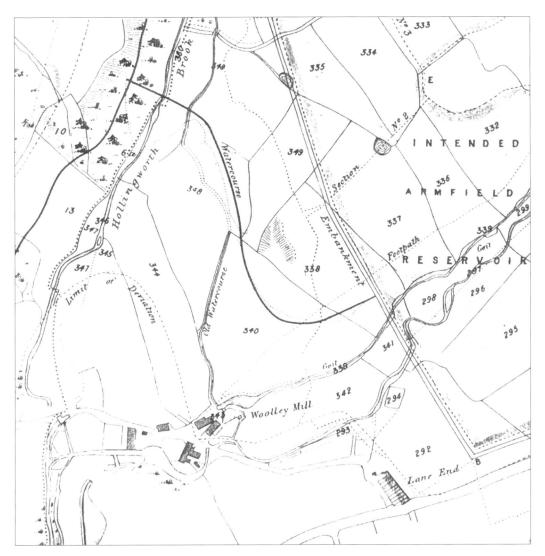

Above: Ordnance Map dated 1846, showing Woolley Mill and its relation to the intended Armfield Reservoir. The mill entrance was in Woolley Mill Lane.

Opposite above: Woolley Mill, Woolley Mill Lane, Tintwistle. Situated opposite Woolley Mill Farm.

Opposite below: Woolley Mill Farm. Farm buildings still in use. Looking west down Woolley Mill Lane. (1A/2)

Millbrook House. Originally a cotton mill, it was converted to its present purpose as a private residence. (1A/3)

Ralph and his family moved into Millbrook House and, later, his cousin James, son of Uncle William, joined them. Millbrook House had beautiful lawns and gardens, and the old goit lodge was transformed into an attractive ornamental lake and fishpond. The house even possessed its own exquisite clock tower, a private chapel, and a huge glass roofed coach-house (which, in around 1960, garaged a magnificent Rolls-Royce Silver Cloud). As James' great interest was meteorology, he installed over £2,000 worth of apparatus and accessories in Millbrook House, and he wrote monthly weather reports for newspapers and journals. Millbrook, both as a mill and residence, had been owned by the Sidebottom family for over 180 years. Mrs Byrom, widow of a Sidebottom, moved out of Millbrook House in about 1970, and the estate was sold to a private buyer.

The Sidebottom Family

Willy Sharpe researched the Sidebottom family, using the Christ Church Tintwistle's *Bazaar Handbook* (1928), in which there is an article written by Colonel William Sidebottom of Harewood, great-grandson of John Sidebottom of Mottram.

Old John Sidebottom lived at Mottram and was a Surveyor Architect and Yeoman, he had a large family, of about twelve children. As the cotton trade was just commencing, he determined to put his sons into one. He bought the Millbrook Waterfall where he built a cotton mill, small at first, but enlarged later, and started two sons there. He also took the Broadbottom Falls, and the sons built Broadbottom Mill. These mills were worked jointly by James, George, Joe, and William. James removed to Millbrook House and Joe and George remained in their family home at Broadbottom while Joe, built Harewood Lodge, and George, built Hill End, as their residence of choice. James bought the Cellar Estate in Hollingworth and built Manor House.

He started his three eldest sons, John, William and James, in business, taking the Waterside Waterfalls and building the mill there. The two younger sons carried on at Millbrook, but one of them died and the other son, Ralph, married and brought up a family there. The second son, William, built Etherow House and lived there until his death in 1870; he had eight children, Tom Harrop, James, William, Anne, Emma, Agnes, Jane, and Lucy. Of these Tom Harrop lived at Etherow House where he died in 1908. James lived at Arrowscroft and then at Millbrook where he died. William and his sister Lucy, lived at Harewood, Broadbottom, where they both died in 1923. Old John Sidebottom died at the grand old age of ninety-two.

And here is the Sidebottom family tree (only sons have been included). The dates and times of births and deaths were obtained by Willy Sharpe from family vaults, tombstones, stained glass windows, and memorials within Christ Church, Tintwistle, and Mottram churchyards:

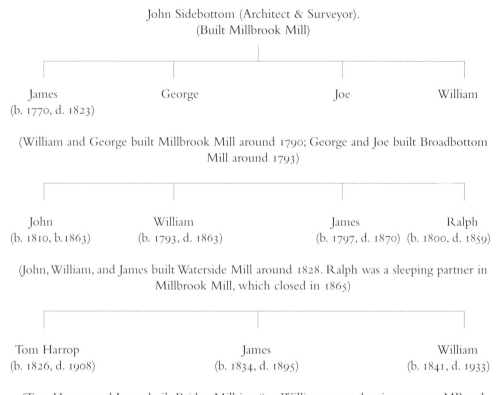

John Sidebottom (Architect & Surveyor).
(Built Millbrook Mill)

James	George	Joe	William
(b. 1770, d. 1823)			

(William and George built Millbrook Mill around 1790; George and Joe built Broadbottom Mill around 1793)

John	William	James	Ralph
(b. 1810, b.1863)	(b. 1793, d. 1863)	(b. 1797, d. 1870)	(b. 1800, d. 1859)

(John, William, and James built Waterside Mill around 1828. Ralph was a sleeping partner in Millbrook Mill, which closed in 1865)

Tom Harrop	James	William
(b. 1826, d. 1908)	(b. 1834, d. 1895)	(b. 1841, d. 1933)

(Tom Harrop and James built Bridge Mill in 1854. William was a sleeping partner, MP, and director of railway company)

The Sidebottom family built Waterside Mills, Bridge Mills, and Millbrook Mill.

Probably the best-known local member of the Sidebottom family was James (1834–1895) who, after being elected on the first Glossop Town Council in 1871, became an alderman a year later. James was Mayor eight times between 1879 and 1888, a period which included Glossop's Jubilee Year. In his first year as Mayor, he presented Glossop with a gold Mayoral chain of office. Brother Tom Harrop Sidebottom was MP for Stalybridge between 1874 and 1880, and then again from 1885 to 1900.

Padfield Brook Mill, Padfield, with Lodge Bank in rear. (1B/7)

Padfield Brook Mill, Padfield, amongst the trees, with Lodge Bank to the right. Note the absence of a chimney, since it was not working as a mill from around 1946. (1B/7)

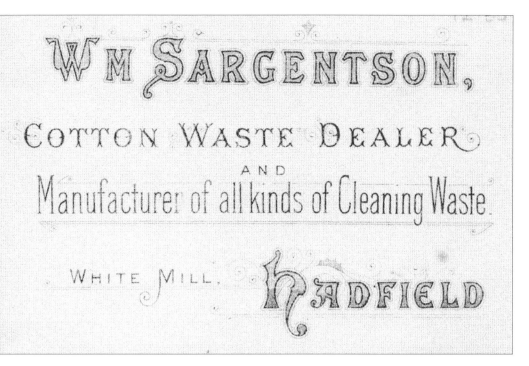

Walter M. Sargentson's calling card. (Courtesy of Sue Hickinson)

Padfield Brook Mill

Constructed in 1807 for cotton spinning, the mill was three storeys high and occupied an area of ¼ acre. It included a lodge and a water turbine. Throughout its existence it operated entirely on water power. John Lees was the first recorded owner in 1828, and he also built his residence, Padfield Brook House, together with Lees Row cottages, which are still in use. On his retirement in 1843, John's son Samuel took over the spinning business and, with a workforce of 103, added weaving looms to manufacture cotton goods. In 1866, the mill changed hands. The new owner was Thomas Platt, who continued the spinning and manufacturing business. Then, in 1878, Edward Platt inherited the mill from his father, and later Edward continued with a partner, James Sargentson Jnr Ltd, and they began dealing in cotton waste. After suffering many setbacks the mill was taken over by Walter M. Sargentson in 1922.

Before the mill ceased trading it had two further owners – Walter F. Sargentson in 1925, and William Sargentson in 1928 – who used the mill solely for dealing in cotton waste. In 1953 the buildings were in a dilapidated condition, as were the lodge and turbine. The mill, at that time, was being used for the storage of cotton waste. The mill was eventually demolished in the 1970s (see photograph, opposite page).

Padfield Mill, Padfield

Date of construction about 1807, for cotton spinning and manufacture. It occupied just over ½ acre of land, plus the mill lodge. First owned for cotton spinning by William Barber in 1828, the name was changed in 1843 to William Barber & Sons. It became a cloth & thread manufacturer in 1849, when the new owners were John Barber & Bros. During 1870, it became the Padfield

Mill Co., controlled by Thomas Rhodes' sons, William and Herbert Rhodes. The Platt family bought the mill in 1876 as William & Edward Platt. In 1881 the owner was Edward Platt & Sons. In 1888, it became Edward Platt & Son. This lasted until 1925 when The Rye Mills Tannery Ltd introduced leather dressing, which continued to flourish, with the last change of ownership – to Joshua Kershaw & Sons – three years later (see photograph, opposite page).

Hadfield Mills, Hadfield

Built originally as a corn mill before 1819, and still in existence as the Hadfield Mill until 1883. In 1874, Thomas Rhodes & Sons converted the mill for the manufacture of cotton. It was an extensive mill, partly four storeys, partly five storeys, occupying an area of over 2½ acres. The mill was supplied with water from a mill pond on the hillside to the south of the mill. In January 1887, the mill had the luxury of a complete installation of electric lights. Between 1884 and 1919, the cotton mill was enlarged and the corn mill disappeared to make way for the new extensions. The founder, Thomas Rhodes, who was from Tintwistle, built his residence, Mersey Bank House, in 1862. By 1873, the mill employed over 1,000 mill-hands and the mill flourished under son W.S. Rhodes. Between 1932 and 1940, the mill was not in use until it was taken over by The Hadfield Worsted Mills Co. Ltd for the manufacture of cloth (see photograph, page 98).

Station Mill, Hadfield

In 1843, Thomas and Edward Platt built this cotton spinning mill. It was partly three storeys high, but mostly single-storey. The buildings alone occupied 1½ acres, and it also had the usual lodge for storing water. On the death of his father in 1870 Edward Platt Jnr inherited the mill, and the mill changed its name to Edward Platt & Sons in 1876. In 1888 it became Edward Platt & Son. Edward Platt was probably the best-known of the Platt family, and he was a shrewd businessman. Although he was a Glossop town councillor for eight years he refused the Mayoralty on the grounds it would take up too much of his time. He was another Glossopdale benefactor, who built Hadfield Library in memory of his father. The Platt family had owned Station Mill for sixty-eight years before selling out in 1923 to E. Willman & Sons, who changed manufacturing from cotton to silk noil spinning and manufacture, and were the last users of the mill prior to demolition.

Edward Platt Jnr erected Hadfield Library as a memorial to his late father and presented it to Glossop Corporation in 1906. After the death of W.S. Rhodes, Edward Platt bought Mersey Bank House and lived there until his death. The mill closed in 1989 (see photograph, page 100).

The White Mill, Hadfield

Constructed about 1807 for cotton manufacture and, in 1828, it was owned jointly by Thomas Thornley and George Platt. It was a small mill occupying only 0.10 acres, with a lodge. It changed hands in 1843, the new owners being William Thomas and Edward Platt. In 1855, Thomas and Edward Platt became owners. Part of the original mill was destroyed by fire and the remainder was used as a farmhouse (see photograph, page 101).

The Red Mill, Hadfield

Very little is known about this mill, except that it was of light construction and had disappeared long before 1954. One lodge, presumed to have been used by the mill, has been filled in.

Padfield Mill, Platt Street. Debris of mill after demolition in 1952, from Padfield, looking east. (1B/9)

Padfield Mill, two years later. Completely demolished, with the Mill Lodge drained. This view is from Temple Street, looking south-west. (1B/9)

Above and below: Station Mill, Hadfield – aerial view of the Platt Family Kingdom.

Opposite above: Hadfield Mills, Hadfield, looking east-south-east up Platt Street, in 1954, when the buildings on the left were still in use, and those on the right were not. Note the branch railway from main line into the old Works Yard. (1B/11)

Opposite below: Hadfield Mills, Hadfield. Taken from the footpath above Platt Street, looking south-south-west. (1B/11)

Station Mill, Hadfield, looking north-east from Platt Street. (1/12)

Station Mill, Hadfield. Rear of mill, looking south-east. Note the emergence of Padfield Brook, which supplied the water power. (1B/12)

The White Mill, 1950. When partly demolished, it was used as a farm. Note Padfield Brook (left), looking south-east, after its passage through and under the mill. (1B/13)

The White Mill. From an engraving from around 1810.

Bridge Mills, Tintwistle. Ruins of spinning mill, looking south-east, in 1953. (2/2)

Bank Bottom, Hadfield

Constructed about 1807 for cotton manufacture, and converted by Henry Wyatt to soap manufacture from 1895 to 1904. The original buildings having been converted into houses.

Bridge Mills, Tintwistle and Hadfield

North and south side of river Etherow, adjoining New Road and across Tintwistle Bridge to Waterside. As with Waterside Mill, Bridge Mill, originally a mill complex of considerable size covering an area of land from buildings alone of 8 acres, was owned by the Sidebottom family.

Built in 1854 for cotton spinning and weaving, the mill was owned by Tom Harrop and James Sidebottom, and formally worked in connection with Waterside Mills on the Hadfield side of the river Etherow. Both mills were about midway between Hadfield and the village of Tintwistle. By 1899, Bridge Mill employed more than 1,000 workers. There were seven Lancashire boilers raising steam for Beam Condensing Engines (representing 1,282hp), including three Gerens patent economisers, and one steam pump. The mills machine power listed 42,746 self-acting weft spindles, 47,888 twist mule spindles, and 2,000 looms. The weekly wage bill, exclusive of staff, amounted to £950 per week and an average weekly wage for an adult expert weaver was about 18s. Bridge Mills extracted water from Padfield Brook, which is augmented by the Torside Clough and also, at that time, by the Tintwistle Waterworks. An auxiliary supply of water for condensing and steam raising was supplied from a pond on the north side of the mills. With the death of James in 1895, the mill changed ownership in 1897, to become Tom Harrop Sidebottom & Co. Ltd.

Bridge Mills Fire, Tintwistle. The disastrous fire of Monday 5 June 1899, looking south-east. (2/2)

Tragedy struck the mill two years later which affected the livelihoods of those in Tintwistle, Hadfield, and Padfield. On a lovely summer's day on Monday 5 June 1899, at about 9.30 a.m., a great fire broke out on the top floor of the mill. The *Glossop Chronicle* reported: 'within a short period from the outbreak, the flames were madly leaping along the top storey of the building, and carrying all before it.' At noontime, the Hollingworth side of the building came crashing down, which gave fresh impetus to the flames, forcing the fire down into the lower floors and Spinning Rooms. The fire soon spread to two large wings of the mill. Hundreds of villagers watched as the fire brigade fought hard to save the huge stone structure, but their efforts proved useless, and most of the rooms were left almost entirely gutted.

The *Glossop Chronicle*, dated Friday 9 June 1899, reported:

We are officially informed that the damage caused by the fire amounts approximately to £45,000, which is covered by insurance. Only recently a great quantity of new carding and other machinery, of the value of several thousand pounds was placed in the mill. Some of this has been saved, but of course a great portion of this has been destroyed. A lot of new cards were uninjured. The engines practically escaped damage. On the Tintwistle side of the building too, the lower rooms escaped with very little damage. Comparatively little damage was done to any of the weaving sheds. Up to the moment of writing, no decision has been arrived at as to the future of the mill but we hear that the question of whether the mill will be rebuilt depends to a large extent on the debenture holders of the company. The wages paid per week, exclusive of managers averages £950, and for some time past the workpeople had earned a very good wage.

On Tuesday morning, the weavers in a shed which was situated a considerable distance from the fire were able to resume work for a short time, but by the end of the year all work ceased. In 1909, the mill was bought by the British Vulcanised Fibre Co. Ltd. for manufacturing fibre board sheets and cylinders. They occupied part of the old weaving section of the mill, which had been built in 1886. The fire also caused the demise of the Sidebottom family's influence on the everyday lives of the people throughout the district, particularly Tintwistle, Padfield, and Hollingworth.

Below are some extracts from Willy Sharpe's notes on an interview with Mr Isaac Ralph of New Road, Tintwistle:

Mr Ralph is a retired draper who was born in Stockport in 1873, and is now eighty years of age. He is in good health and has a remarkable memory. He appeared to enjoy speaking of bygone times and the industries in this locality. At the age of twelve, Mr Isaac commenced work from 1885, at Sidebottom's Waterside and Bridge Mills, to shortly after the tragic Bridge Mill fire in 1899. Owing to Sidebottom's mill closing down entirely, he had to seek other employment. Due to the noise experienced whilst working in the weaving sheds he now wears a hearing aid. Mr Ralph gave me the following information regarding the weaving portion of Waterside Mills where he worked:

Bridge Mills, Tintwistle – former weaving sheds, occupied in 1953 by British Vulcanised Fibre Co., who built additional sheds to replace those lost in the fire of 1899. (2/2)

Name of weaving shed	Approx. number of looms
Chimney Shed	1,000
Garden Shed	400
Old Shed	600
Crystal Palace Shed	100
New Mill Bottom Shed	100
New River Shed	500
Old River Shed	500
Approx. total number of looms	3,200

New River Shed and Old River Shed were situated alongside the river immediately on the Hadfield side of Tintwistle Bridge. The culvert from the inlet sluices flowing out of the river ran through one of these sheds on its way to the turbine. This turbine was in operation and working at Waterside through to 1895. Mr Ralph also states that apart from New River Shed and Old River Shed this huge mill had been idle for four years at the time of the Bridge Mill fire, and the best of the machinery and the most modern at the time had been taken out and transferred to Bridge Mill when Gartside and Co. (of Manchester) Ltd bought from Sidebottoms at Bridge Mill the looms, slashing, winding, warping, machines and carding engines, which were taken back from Bridge Mill and installed in Waterside Mill. Mr Ralph said that, on the morning of Bridge Mill fire, he had been told to help install new carding engines in the Bridge Mill card-room, but the fire upset these arrangements and the carding engines were ultimately removed to Waterside. At the time of the Bridge Mills fire, Mr Ralph, along with other expert male weavers, was engaged in weaving on a type of very fast and powerful loom, known locally as 'Hell Fire Jacks'. On these looms it was possible to earn almost one pound per week. In their weaving sheds they had a production board, on which was entered the names, quantities and wages, by the best ten weavers week by week, the most consistent weavers earning small bonuses at pastimes and festival seasons, such as Wakes Week, Christmas, etc. This led to a spirit of rivalry and intense competition amongst the more expert and skilled of the male weavers, for the honour of being known as 'the best weaver in the shed'.

Mr Ralph also recalls that there was a carved inscription on the wall of the stone weaving shed which read: 'Jepson – sign teetotal 1847'. There was also a drawing of a heart and a duck but no one ever knew the meaning, it was anybody's guess. In the spring of 1900, Gartside and Co. Ltd, of Manchester, came to Waterside Mills bringing with them their key operatives and equipment and their key operatives and cotton machinery from their mills in the Ardwick district; Waterside was again back in production. At first they wove satins and damasks and other materials described by one of their earliest employed weavers as 'fancies'. During the mill's history it had manufactured Rayon, Crepe de Chine, Fancy Figured Cloths, Marocains, Piques, Poplins, Pyjama Cloths, Rayon Fabrics, Shirtings, Spun Rayon, and even Typewriter Cloth. (End of interview)

Waterside Mills, Hadfield and Tintwistle.

Waterside Mills, on the southern bank of the river Etherow, built in 1777 by John Turner and John Thornley for cotton spinning and weaving, was originally named Brookside Mill, and was to eventually become the largest group of mills in the district. On the dissolution of the Waterside partnership following the death of John Thornley Snr in 1791, his son Robert Thornley was denied partnership. John Thornley had not willed it that Robert would become part of the former partnership between himself and his partner John Turner, but willed that Robert would benefit by being entitled to have equal share to all profits and materials in process at that time, which was quite substantial. John Thornley Snr was a much respected man and over 300 people, many of them his mill-hands, attended his funeral. By 1828, Waterside had changed ownership and was owned by John and William Sidebottom, of Millbrook House, and the company was named John William Sidebottom & Co. The mill, occupied by buildings alone, was 8 acres, and most of the mill buildings were five storeys high, employing 835 mill-hands. A weir had been constructed across the whole width of the river Etherow with large sluices for the diversion of water to a goit, leading to a large waterwheel which powered the mill machinery.

Waterside Mill also possessed an auxiliary water supply from Padfield Brook. Later, with the advent of steam power, the waterwheel was replaced by large turbines with steam raising and condensing facilities. In 1868, a fire of considerable magnitude occurred but, although it slowed down production, the mill continued working. By 1890, the mill employed over 2,000 employees, working 3,200 looms. On the death of James Sidebottom in 1895, all work ceased, through lack of business, and the mill was closed down.

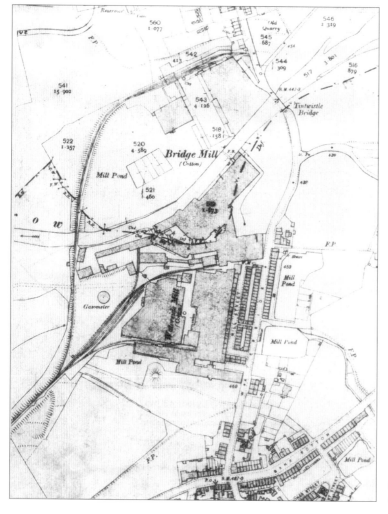

Location map, 1890, showing Bridge Mill and Waterside Mill.

Waterside Mills, Hadfield and Tintwistle. Five storey mill, looking north from Woolley Bridge Road. (2/3)

Waterside Mills, Hadfield and Tintwistle. Weir across river Etherow for diverting water via the mill sluices to the mill goit, leading to original waterwheel. Note the mill sluices and control valves in stone wall. (2/3)

Waterside Mills, Hadfield and Tintwistle. Facing west-north-west, the five-storey building on the right was used as a store by Maconochie's Ltd (2/3).

In 1916, a disused part of Waterside was taken over by Greenfield Mill Co. Ltd, who described themselves as bleachers. During the First World War, part of the remaining mill building was used as a munitions factory, making gun cotton and other similar materials for armament purposes. Settling ponds of earthen construction had to be built to use in the converting of cotton waste into gun cotton. The ponds were used to settle suspended solids after processing had been completed. The water used for this process was taken from Padfield Brook via Torside Goit. Subsequently to processing, it was then returned to the settling ponds. The description of the premises as 'bleachers' was probably for security reasons. Willy Sharpe remembers the strict guard that was kept by uniformed policemen on each entrance, and the search made of the workers for matches, tobacco, etc., before they were allowed into the works. When the war ended, Greenfield Mill Co. Ltd, bleachers, quietly faded away. During the mill's history it had manufactured rayon, crepe di chine, fancy figured cloths, piques, poplins, pyjama cloths, rayon fabrics, shirtings, spun rayon, and even typewriter cloth. There were 1,000 people employed at the mill during 1926. This dwindled to 800 in 1935 and, by 1953, was down to 700 employees.

In 1940, parts of Waterside Mills were taken over by Maconochie's Foodstuffs Ltd, who manufactured tinned and bottled pickles, sauces, soups, vegetables, meats, etc. Maconochie's had been bombed out of their previous premises and, in 1941, they established themselves at the mill by reconstructing a total area of 2½ acres, of single-storey building of light construction. They employed over 500 workers. Of the original mill, approximately one-third had been demolished and, by 1954, further demolition occurred, with about half of the original magnificent mill building still in use by other smaller companies. In 1976, further demolition and restructuring of the site took place. The site was eventually developed, and named the Hadfield Trading Estate.

Too much common sense and imagination would have been required by the High Peak District Council to have retained and included the historic name, i.e. Waterside Mills Trading

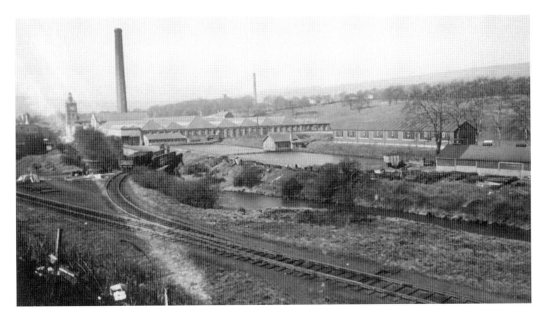

River Etherow Bleaching Co. Ltd, Hollingworth. On the site of the former Dalton's Print Works. General view of works looking west, showing both the works and lodges. River Etherow in the foreground. (2/4)

Estate, Hadfield. This would have been a fitting tribute to all those mill-workers who lived, breathed, and worked in one of the largest cotton mills in Derbyshire.

River Etherow Bleaching Co. Ltd, Hollingworth

Formerly Dalton's Print Works (as shown above), it was built before 1816 for calico printing and dyeing, and was situated 1 mile downstream from Bottoms Reservoir. From 1928, it was owned by John and Thomas Dalton, in 1865 it was John Dalton's, and it remained in the Dalton family until 1872, when it was bought out by The River Etherow Bleaching Co. Ltd for bleaching and finishing. The original building works completely disappeared when the River Etherow Bleaching Co. reconstructed the site. By 1930, there were 1,100 employees, and by 1953 this number had reduced to 228 employees.

Further extracts from Mr Charles Wilson's diaries during 1853 refer to visits to Rhodes Wood, accompanied by Mr Dalton, the print works owner:

Monday 26 May 1853
Go to Rhodes Wood Reservoir inspecting dirty water at Daltons.

Saturday 4 June 1853
Afterwards go with Mr Dalton to Rhodes Wood inspecting river water being made very turbid by Works there.

Thursday 6 October 1853
Return by 4.30 train to Hadfield, ride home in Mr John Dalton's cab (Expenses – to Mr Dalton's coachman – 5p)

River Etherow Bleach Works, looking south-east. The picture shows the admin offices and part of the works (left), and a building occupied in 1950 by John Walton of Glossop (right). Note boundary plate reading 'R.E.B. Co.' (left foreground, near road gully).

COTTON MILLS AND PAPER MILLS OF GLOSSOP

Woollen mills were functioning in Glossop as early as the late sixteenth century but it was not until the 1800s that Glossopdale began to rely commercially on its development as a cotton town. There were fourteen cotton mills in the 1780s, by the 1830s this had increased to thirty mills, and, fifty years later, there were over forty-five cotton mills, with three of the mills being the biggest and finest developed mills in the country.

Hawkshead, Starkies, or Roofless Mill

Built in 1783 on Blackshaw Clough by William Sheppard, one of the first mill-owners in the area, and originally a fustian manufacturer. By the late 1770s, he favoured fabrics made entirely of cotton, and built Hawkshead Mill, off Hope Street, Old Glossop, employing ten mill-hands. The mill became so successful that he was able to accumulate enough wealth to build other mills in Glossopdale. A lease, dated 29 September, 1791, was taken out by a James Starkie, a merchant from Manchester who remained a successful cotton spinner until his death in 1830, aged sixty-three. By 1823, the tenants were Messrs Benjamin Rolfe & Bubb, who were so successful that, by 1828, they registered 9,336 spindles. When Rolfe became sole owner in March of the same year, he changed the name to Roofless Mill. He was also a tenant of Shepley's Mill. Rolfe was known to be very warm-hearted and it is related that he would place apples on a wall to tempt children to take them. If a child scrummed one he would shout after the culprit to frighten him or her out of their skin, but if the child passed by he would reward the child for their honesty. Rolfe died on 25 March 1830, aged sixty-three. The owners in 1828 were Messrs Waterhouse and Holland, boasting 11,370 spindles and, by 1831, Waterhouse became the sole tenant, further increasing the business within twelve months to 13,608 spindles and 128 looms. The mill burnt down in 1837, but was rebuilt within a year by Messrs Joseph Berresford and John Holland. Part of the old Roofless Mill in Wesley Street was converted into cottages, which still exist opposite the school.

Mersey Mills, Woolley Bridge, Glossop

Constructed in 1846 on the south bank of the river Etherow for cotton spinning and weaving, and owned by Thomas Rhodes & Sons Ltd from 1846 to 1928. The old building was 2½ acres in area and the spinning mill was four storeys high, plus the basement. The mill included weaving sheds, a Ring Room, and a boiler house, with steam raising and condensing facilities. In 1928, the mill was purchased by Lancashire Cotton Corporation and retained by them until 1934. They also owned parts of the spinning mill (four storeys and a basement), old weaving sheds, large weaving sheds, Ring Room, warehouse, boiler, and engine house, etc. By 1953, the occupiers or owners were as follows:

(a) J.G. Webbing Ltd – weavers producing webbing and military equipment, employing forty people. It was part of the old premises know as the 'The New Shed' (it was nine bays in extent, one storey high).

(b) Part of the old premises, known as 'The Small Shed', belonged to Hadfield Silks Ltd, producing silk and rayon fabrics and novelties. They employed forty people and had 120 spindles and sixty looms in six bays of one storey high. There was also a two-storey office block.

(c) John Walton (of Glossop) Ltd, bleaching and finishing, owned a new block of single-storey sheds on the site of the old spinning mill and old weaving shed. It included a mechanic's shop and loading bays, and a former extension to Mersey Mills known as Winding Rooms or Beaming Rooms of two storeys high. They also built and occupied a new shed outside the area of the mill by the side of Woolley Bridge Road.

Mersey Mills, Hollingworth. The entrance shows the last extension of the original mills, built in 1912 on the site of the Old Spinning Mill and Old Weaving Shed. There is a railway crossing in the foreground. The chimney smokes, and all is well. (2/5/A)

Mersey Mills, Hollingworth, looking north-west. Part of the old weaving sheds, called the 'Small Sheds' (single-storey, nine bays in extent), shown on right of picture, were occupied by Hadfield Silks Ltd, and the lower ones to the left by Webbing Weavers (JG) Ltd. The buildings in the background, the clock tower, and the chimney, belong to the River Etherow Bleaching Co. Ltd. (2/5/B)

Turn Lee Paper Mill, Glossop

One of the largest paper mills in the North of England. The paper trade was introduced into Glossop in 1833. Turn Lee is first mentioned in a directory of 1848, as owned by Samuel Kershaw & Co. (cotton spinners, paper makers, and cotton wool carders). In 1870, Turn Lee was owned by T.H. Ibbotson, paper makers. The mill changed ownership in 1873, when it was purchased by Edward Partington. In 1878, E. Ritter and Carl Kellner perfected 'the sulphite process', considerably reducing the time taken in the pulping process by admitting steam direct to digestion. In 1885, the process was first introduced to America. Edward Partington became associated with Kellner, as Partington & Kellner; and the process caused a revolution in the paper trade. Turn Lee Paper Mill adopted this process and manufactured up to 120 tons of paper per week, employing 600 workers, in addition to a large administration staff. The new process made Partington and Kellner very wealthy men.

The mills worked continuously from Sunday night until Saturday morning on the production of paper. Saturdays and Sundays were used to clean and maintain machinery and premises. The accumulated waste china clay, which was used as a filter in the process of paper-making, was discharged into the Chunal Brook every Saturday morning. Another change took place in 1876, when the firm became Olive & Partington, then again in 1954, when it was Olive & Partington Ltd, a subsidiary of the Inveresk Paper Co. Ltd (of which Kellner Partington was also a subsidiary). Turn Lee closed down in 1961.

Edward Partington, the man who built an empire at Turn Lee, was born in 1836, and moved to Glossop in 1863. He was renowned to visit the mill regularly, even though he owned paper mills and lumber forests all over the world. He became a distinguished benefactor to Glossop giving £30,000 to build a Convalescent and Nurses Home. He also gave a donation of £2,000 towards the Victoria Hall and built a new pavilion for the Glossop Cricket Club. Edward Partington, Baron Doverdale of Westwood, MP, JP, died in 1836.

Longdendale Works, Woolley Bridge (John Walton of Glossop Ltd)

Constructed around 1910 on the south bank of the river Etherow, mostly in Glossop, for the River Etherow Bleaching Co. Ltd, comprising one long single-storey shed, and another single-storey shed divided into a number of bays so as to form an L-shaped building. In 1949, the premises were leased out to John Walton of Glossop Ltd, a subsidiary of Tootal Broadhurst Lee and Co. Ltd, for bleaching and finishing. They also owned the rights to one-quarter of the water abstracted from the river by the Lessors for steam raising, etc. In 1953, they employed approximately 330 people. The old part of the works remained as built in 1910 but, since being taken over by John Walton, new buildings were added during 1951 and 1952 (see photograph overleaf).

Woolley Bridge Mill or Lees Mill

On the east bank of the river Etherow in the angle of Woolley Lane and Glossop Road. Built and owned in 1825 by Henry Lees for cotton spinning, while his younger brother John (later, both John and Edward) owned the Padfield Brook Lees Mill, a medium-sized stone-built mill with sheds occupying ½ acre. In the 1840s they employed over 200 mill-hands. The mill's name was changed to Henry Lees & Son in 1870, when the son came into partnership with his father and, six years later, Robert Lees was the recorded mill-owner. After fifty-three years ownership the Lees sold Woolley Bridge Mill to George Fawcett in 1881, who changed the cotton spinning mill to basket and skip manufacture. In 1890, the mill became an ironworks, when it was purchased by Roberts Bros & Co. In 1903, the mill became a dye works, the same year as enforced short-time employment brought on by a cotton shortage. The curtain went up in 1908, when part of the mill became the Woolley Bridge Variety Palace. In 1912, it became a cinema before the lights finally went out in 1925 (see photograph on page 115).

Longdendale Works, Woolley Bridge (John Walton of Glossop Ltd), looking west. End of weaving sheds on Woolley Bridge Road, looking west. Now demolished and replaced by modern industrial site units. (2/6)

Longdendale Works, Woolley Bridge. New extensions to existing Longdendale Works, as in 1953, built by Messrs John Walton of Glossop Ltd. (2/6)

Woolley Bridge Mill, or Lee's Mill, Brookfield – all that remained in 1953 of a once fair-sized mill. Looking west-south-west along the Glossop Road. (2/7)

It appears from a photograph taken in 1953 that the mill had become mostly demolished, with only the mill chimney, and one part of the mill near the roadside, shown to be still remaining.

Brookfield Mill, or Shepley's Mill, Glossop

In his early forties, Samuel Shepley had the mill built (in 1818) for cotton spinning and weaving. The making of the branch highway from the Plough Inn to the Spreadeagle Inn had already led to the development of Brookfield and Woolley Bridge. The son of Samuel's brother John, Joshua Shepley, built the Royal Oak, when the highway to Sheffield had recently opened. The mill was bounded by the Hollingworth to Glossop Road, a fairly large mill of 1 acre, situated in the easterly angle of the confluence of the Glossop Brook and the river Etherow. John had a unique experience while he was reconstructing the mill goit channel to the mill reservoir. He discovered a stone coffin in which was buried a Roman soldier, one of a garrison at the adjoining Roman fort. In the coffin was a silver coin of the Roman Emperor, Domitien, A.D. 81–96. The coin was loaned to a person for valuation but was never returned.

In 1831, according to the *Manchester Guardian*, Mr Samuel Shepley, father to John and William, had an unfounded charge made against him:

On Tuesday last, August 31st at the New Bailyee (Manchester), an informer named Davis summoned Mr Samuel Shepley, of Brookfield, charging him with having a one horse cart, loaded with cotton, in Market Street, Manchester, on the 17th inst., no place of residence being visible on the name plate. In answer to a question from Mr Shepley, Davis said it was a narrow wheeled cart, drawn by a black horse. In defence, Mr Shepley stated he had no cart narrower than 6in wheels, and that all his horses were bay or brown; and that he had no cart in Manchester on the day in question. The case was accordingly dismissed.

Brookfield Mill or Shepley's Mill. Remains of the mill frontage alongside the Glossop Road at Brookfield, around 1953. (2/8)

Glory days of Brookfield Mill or Shepley's Mill. This newspaper cutting was taken from the *Glossop Chronicle & Advertiser* for week ending Friday 26 June 1953, when Brookfield Mill was in full working order. In background of procession can be seen Brookfield Mills (now demolished). (2/8)

The fall of Brookfield or Shepley's Mill chimney. Demolished by the famous 'Blaster' Bates on 24 August 1935.

Samuel Shepley died on 11 December 1858, and his sons, John and William, continued the business, following in their father's footsteps. John Shepley became councillor for the Hadfield Ward. He died on 6 July 1876, aged sixty-five. William Shepley was also a member of the Glossop Town Council, for the Hadfield Ward, and at the first Glossop Council Elections, he was made an alderman. He was Mayor between 1868 and 1870, and was one of the first seven borough magistrates, appointed on 12 June 1853. He chaired the Board of Guardians for many years and, on retirement, he was presented with a £50 gold watch at the Station Inn, of which he was very proud. Sadly, he was robbed of it while attending a Liberal demonstration at Chatsworth House. In September 1886, in recognition of long services rendered to the Liberal Party, he was presented with a silver salver at New Mills Public Hall. In 1888, William turned the business into a limited company: J&W Shepley Ltd. William Shepley died on 7 May 1889, aged seventy-five. William's nephew, William Shepley Rhodes Esq., JP, was another member of the celebrated Rhodes family. By 1900, Shepley's Mills operated a record 43,000 spindles, a figure never to be equalled again.

In the winter of 1911–12, a great part of the mill was destroyed by a huge fire and, although, around 1927, a Belgium firm refurbished the mill and installed elaborate machinery, strangely enough production on any scale never materialised. An entry in Kelly's Directory of Derbyshire for 1925, is given as: 'Walter Stockdale, Printer, Brookfield Mill'. It was the first and only entry for this firm.

By 1940, the once proud Brookfield Mill had been demolished, and the site was leased to the Brookside Grit Co., who produced and sold poultry grit until 1948. The Shepleys would have turned in their graves! This was followed, in July 1953, by the use of part of the old mill as a garage and car-wreckers yard, littered with dumped cars. A motor coach standing in the yard read: 'Melandra Coaches Ltd'.

Bankwood Works, Broadbottom, sometimes called Botany Works. The river Etherow is behind the works. (2/11)

Bankwood Works, or Botany Works, near Broadbottom

William Wardlow built Bankwood, in 1828, for cotton spinning and weaving. It was an extensive mill, occupying 1 acre of buildings, and was possibly built in instalments, as part-stone and part-brick. It had a weir constructed across the river with a head goit, and the machinery was eventually powered by a large water turbine. It was passed on to James William Wardlow in 1834, before he sold it in 1848 to Ralph Waller & Co. It again changed owners to the Bankwood Spinning Co. Ltd in 1876. The mill progressed to calico printing in 1890, when it was bought by Yates and Kay. In about 1935, it became George Kay & Co. During the First World War the mill closed down. It was later occupied by Messrs E.P. Bray and Co., manufacturing pigments (dyestuffs). The last known owner, in around 1953, was Messrs Keiner & Co. Ltd, of Coomes Lane Works, Charlesworth, who manufactured pigments for the paint and leather trades.

Best Hill Mills, or Marsland Mills, Broadbottom

A very old masonry cotton spinning mill built in 1793, with buildings occupying ½ acre. The owner was Kelsall & Marsland. The mill had two waterwheels, one 12ft in diameter and 12ft wide, and the other 15ft in diameter and 12ft wide. Both wheels were powered by water supplied via two weirs constructed across the river. The mill passed on to Samuel Marsland in 1828–1855, then became John Marsland & Brother in 1878. They also owned Lymefield Mill. The mill began manufacturing tape about 1919, when Patent Loom & Tape Co. Ltd became proprietors. The reputed owner in 1949 was Mr S. Turner of Glossop, possessing thirty-six Braiding Machines, manufacturing braided cordage. Between 1952 and 1953, its name was changed to Besthill Braids & Cortege Ltd (see photographs on pages 120-121).

Lymefield Mill

A steam-powered cotton spinning mill, built before 1872, and owned in 1878 by John Marsland & Bros. It was a fairly large cotton spinning and doubling mill, comprising four large bays of three storeys, and one of three storeys, within ½ acre, excluding the weir, etc. Edward Platt & Son became new owners in 1892 and worked the mill until 1902, before an unrecorded four-year period of uncertainty, when Broad Mills Co. Ltd purchased the mill in 1906, and worked it until 1934. The last known owners were Cairo Mills Ltd, of Waterhead, Oldham. Cottonspinning and doubling continued for a time, and was still in active work and in good condition under leasehold up to 1953 (see photographs on page 122).

Broad Mills, or Broadbottom Mills

Original mills constructed about 1793, of nearly 2 acres, for George and Joe Sidebottom. Later, they added a further 1½ acres of land, to create newer mills. George was one of the original mill-owners who objected to the construction of the Longdendale Reservoirs. By this time they employed 850 people working 25,000 spindles and 1,500 looms. John Sidebottom took over in 1850, and extended the mill to receive 1,000 additional looms. The steam power at the mills was equal to 240hp. Broad Mills dominated the township of Broadbottom and, at its peak, employed 1,200 workers. John Sidebottom sold out to John Hirst & Sons in 1872. In 1889, it was bought by Broadbottom Mills Co. Ltd who, by 1906, also owned Lymefield Mill. Broadbottom Mills Co. Ltd worked it until 1902.

As with Lymefield Mill, no records were available for four years, until it too was taken over by Broad Mills Co. Ltd in 1906. All went well until 1934, when the firm was forced to go into liquidation. The plant was sold off piecemeal. The mill buildings were sold in 1938 to O.L. Speeding, Eagle Ironworks, Stalybridge. In 1949, the mills were almost completely demolished, and the land was used for keeping poultry and pigs and for the storage of old motor car tyres. In 1953, the site was part-occupied by A.E. Hemsworth, rubber reclamation, formerly of Mersey Mills, Hadfield (see photographs on pages 122-123).

Hodge Mill, Moss Mill, or Bridge Mill, Broadbottom

This was situated on the west bank of the Etherow, 120 yards upstream of the Charlesworth Brook. When it was first built, in around 1796, it was a very small self-contained mill, owned by Moss Bros as a woollen mill, with a farm attached. According to the Longdendale Urban District Council's Sales Plan, 1796, 'Moss Mill was leased for 99 years, in 1805 the mill was again leased out for 90 years'.

In Pigot's Directory of 1828, we read: 'Samuel Becket, Cotton Spinner, Hodge Hall Mill. In 1813, the site was also registered as a bleaching factory.' In 1828, the mill was owned by Samuel and Joseph Beckett, who converted the mill to manufacture cotton. James Radley became the new owner in 1847, and continued with cotton manufacturing, in addition to calico printing. When John Jackson purchased the mill in 1872, he introduced spinning, until he ceased trading in 1878. The mill is now completely demolished and, apart from the remains of the goit, there is no trace of buildings of any kind.

Above: Best Hill Mills or Marsland Mills, Broadbottom. A reproduction from an old engraving of 1794, showing Best Hill Mills original premises as seen through the arch of the bridge. A typical example of a cotton mill of the early Industrial Revolution period, designed for entire operation by water power. (2/12)

Opposite above: Best Hill Mills or Marsland Mills, Broadbottom, as seen through two of the masonry pillars of the railway viaduct of the Best Hill (Broadbottom Arches) around 1928.

Opposite below: Best Hill Mill or Marsland Mill, Broadbottom. This was all that remained of the mill in 1954, when it was still being used by a small braiding firm, whose motive power was electricity.

Lymefield Mill, Broadbottom. The river Etherow is on the far side. (2/13)

Broad Mills or Broadbottom Mills. The works in its prime, looking north. This was a very extensive group of mills, working until 1934. Weaving sheds are to the right. The river Etherow may be discerned in front of the mills. (2/14)

Broad Mills or Broadbottom Mills, looking south-east. On the right of the picture, the river Etherow flows through the power house.

Broad Mills or Broadbottom Mills. Comprehensive view of the site and ruins from lane leading from Well Row to Summerbottom, looking south-east. The space covered with bushes was occupied by the mills. Ruined weaving sheds may be seen in the background (right). (2/14)

Hodge Printworks, Broadbottom. View of the ruins from the Derbyshire bank of the river Etherow, looking west. Note the large weir, sluices, and outlet culvert of tailrace. (2/15)

Hodge Printworks, Broadbottom

Hodge Mill was first established around 1763 as a woollen mill, and is one of the earliest mills in the area. The mill was sub-let for calico printing to Samuel Matley & Son from 1805 until 1872. It had extensive premises and the building alone occupied rather more than 1½ acres. It possessed three reservoirs on the north side of Hodge Lane, and had a weir and sluices constructed across the river Etherow, the water being conveyed by tunnel to the lodges. Two waterwheels, each of 12ft diameter and 12ft width, supplied the power capable of producing up to 40hp. The works had steam raising and condensing facilities and water was used extensively in the processing applications. From about 1835, it boasted its own gasworks to light up the site. A year later it was converted from cotton manufacturing to printing, and renamed Hodge Printworks, employing an average work force of 200 people operating fourteen printing machines. Ledeboer Bros & Co. became owners in 1872, before being taken over by Milner, Gibson & Costabadie in 1889, who introduced dyeing (indigo). The works became Gibson & Costabadie in 1890, and they retained the calico printing. It was then sold to Harry Alister Constable in 1902. This was a branch of CPA, who eventually closed down the plant in 1901. The site was partially demolished from about 1917 to 1919, and completely demolished by 1953.

Wren Nest Mill, aerial view. (Photo courtesy of *Glossop Chronicle*, 24 February 1978)

Dinting Vale Print Works and Lodge, Glossop.

Jubilee Mill, Turnlee

Built in 1887, during the year of Queen Victoria's Golden Jubilee. Closed down in the early 1960s, when part of it was demolished.

Wren Nest Mills

This was a cotton mill originally built by Lord Howard and later sold to the Ellison family. In October 1822, Francis Sumner moved to Glossop to join his stepmother's family, a branch of the Ellisons. On the Wren Nest site he built a six-storey cotton mill and warehouses. In its heyday the mill employed 1,400 mill-workers, operating 123,000 spindles and 2,541 looms. After being damaged by fire the mill never fully recovered. The mill ceased trading in 1955.

Dinting Vale Printworks

Built originally by Joseph Lyne for spinning and carding. The mill was left empty for many years until Edmund Potter, the founder, rebuilt the mill in 1825, and redeveloped it as a printworks. By 1883, with a workforce of 350 workers, it had printed 1 million pieces on forty-two machines. The works closed down in around 1966, and the two mill chimneys were demolished later by 'Blaster' Bates.

As the name John Wood appears so often in the history of the mills of Glossop, this short biography may be helpful in understanding his character, and the number of mills the family owned. John Wood was born in Marsden, Yorkshire, in 1785, but little is known of his earlier days and education, although it was said he was a beautiful writer, a bookkeeper, and a well-versed letter writer. His brothers shared ownership in Narrow Mill, but nothing more is known about them, suggesting that they were John Wood's 'sleeping partners'. John married a Liverpool lady whose maiden name was Hill, and by whom he had three sons and two daughters: John, Eliza, Daniel, Samuel, and Alice. Before venturing to Glossop, he lived in Manchester and Liverpool, from where he acquired his knowledge of spinning and weaving. There was a ridiculous old wives' tale that circulated in Glossop for a time: 'When he first came to Glossop he could ill afford either a pair of shoes or clogs but wore one of each on his feet.'

This theory was dispelled when it was learned that John Wood, who was almost thirty years of age at the time, had leased three empty cotton mills in Old Glossop, in 1815, including Thread Mill, for which he paid a rental of £478 per annum, and Old Water Mill, at a rental of £88 per annum, which included a residence in Hope Street, Glossop. These mills were owned by Mr Robert Bennett, a cotton spinner from Mottram. This alone proved he must have had money and assets and support from his bank. His first year's cotton production was on sale from 7 November 1815 and, by 1816, he was dealing with twenty-two firms, with transactions amounting to over £30,000 per annum. From one firm alone he sold over £6,000 worth of goods. Two years later John Wood rented New Water Mill and Warhurst Meadow from Mr Bennett at £211 per annum and, on instalment of extra Mules, which commenced work on 20 November 1821, the rent was increased to £264.

John Wood's diligence and eye for business, combined, later, with help from his sons – Daniel, Samuel and John – resulted in a colossal mill empire. They are credited with creating Howard Town – one of the largest cotton mill complexes in the country. By 1895, Howard Town Mills covered an area of 14 acres, boasted 221,000 spindles and 3,500 looms and, when in full operation, secured work for over 5,000 people.

Although of different religions and fierce rivals, two of John Wood's sons married the daughters of William Sidebottom of Waterside, thus uniting two of the area's most powerful mill-owning families. John Wood Jnr built their family home in Whitfield, and it was named Whitfield House. The Wood family have the distinction of building and endowing both Wood's

Samuel Hill Wood and his son, Samuel Jnr. He was the third son of John Wood, of Howard Town Mills, 1819–88 (courtesy of Glossop Heritage).

Hospital and the Municipal Baths. They also paid for the laying out of Manor Park, Glossop, on land that was gifted to Glossop by Lord Howard.

When Samuel Snr's wife, Ann Kershaw, became a widow, she found herself as the head of the family. A woman of boundless energy, Ann Kershaw became Glossop's first Lady Freeman. Her son Samuel became an MP, and later, together with his cousin John, a Baron.

The Hope, Top, Higher Water, Barracks, or Wards Mill

Many mills change their name when new owners move in, and this is a typical example. The mill was first occupied by John Wood in 1815, when he first came to Glossop. When he sold the mill, it was assessed as having 5,280 spindles. Samuel Collier was the manager at the time and he later moved on as manager of Wren Nest Mills. He was also a clockmaker, and many of his clocks were sold locally. Some, no doubt, will still be ticking away in Glossop homes and beyond. The mill was purchased by Sale & Harrison in 1830 but lay empty until 1831, when Benjamin Waterhouse, who was at the time the sole tenant of Roofless Mill, worked it in conjunction with Lower Water Mill. Benjamin Waterhouse was known to be a skilled yet reckless horseman who travelled most days to Manchester, and he would generally accomplish the distance, either way, within the hour. In 1846, Messrs Berresford & Holland became tenants, followed by T.P. Sykes & Sons. The mill burned down in 1875.

Chew Wood Mill – Chisworth

Built in 1795. Managed by the Rowbottom family on a ninety-nine-year lease. It was initially used for carding and scrubbing wool and employed twelve to fourteen workers (mostly women and children). The overflow water from the Alma Coal Pit on Sandy Lane fed the mill pond to drive the waterwheel to supply power for the machines. During the Boer War (1899–1902), khaki cloth for the military uniforms, etc., was dyed at the mill. The mill pond was badly flooded during the great flood in June 1930, and was subsequently closed down later in the 1930s. The mill was eventually demolished, in around 1962.

Thread Mill

Built in around 1790 on leased land owned by Mr Benjamin Goodison and bounded by Tanyard Meadow on the Hurst Brook. The mill also bounded the Sheffield Road leading to Mossy Lea. By 1823, John Wood was working it, and occupied both the mill and the adjoining house. The mill made bobbins, hat tips and doubled yarn for hand-loom workers. Mr Wood travelled weekly to Huddersfield, carrying his work on his back. He remained at the mill until July 1840, when he moved to Mouse Nest Mill at Padfield. Thread Mill remained empty for six years until John Wood started his wadding business. Later, the mill was taken over as a brewery by a Mr Greaves, but later still reverted to a mill, manufacturing tape and banding. The house was reputed to have been employed as a cottage hospital for smallpox patients, and some believe it became Harrop's Chapel for nonconformists, which, at that time, was frowned upon. The mill ceased working from around 1899.

Cowbrook Mill

William Hadfield, a roller turner of Hadfield, obtained a lease of land – Meadow Warth, Sheffield Road – on 30 May 1801. It was bounded on the east by the Little Ford, and partly on the south by Scotland Brook. On 7 December, a new lease was obtained for 999 years and, by 1824, the mill was working 4,656 spindles. On 22 June 1843, William Hadfield died, aged seventy-six. His son John took control and continued the business until his death on 22 June 1876, when John's son,

Meadow Mills, Shepley Street, Old Glossop. Established 1877 as a cotton mill by Samuel Rowbottom, who also manufactured cotton ropes, bands, and tape.

Joshua Henry, inherited the business and continued his calling until his death in January 1906. The mill had been in the Hadfield family for ninety-eight years before being sold to Edward Platt, JP, of Mersey Bank (also a joint owner of Padfield Mill, Station Mill, The White Mill, and Lymefield Mill). Edward also took over the lease of the Torside Goit, from his father, until 1890.

The Grove Mill, or Silk Mill, or Meadow Mills

(Photograph above). Possibly also named Meadow Mills. Built by Robert Shepley of Shepley Street, as a cotton mill, in 1825, it also manufactured cotton ropes, bands, and tape. At one time it was managed by Ben James Wilkinson, who learned the trade of cotton spinning from Francis J. Sumner and his cousin John Shepley. Ben lived in a house adjoining the mill which, because of its irregular shape, was nicknamed the 'Old Salt Box'.

In 1925, Grove Mill became a silk mill and changed its name, accordingly, to Silk Mill. It was occupied by James Bosley, Smith, Bosley & Co., manufacturing silk ribbons, etc. In 1838, a robbery took place, and this was reported on 7 June in the *Stockport Advertiser*:

> On Saturday morning, a watchman saw two men in the street at Glossop, with bundles in their arms, he seized both, but one got away with a bundle. It was discovered that Bosley's Silk Mill had been robbed of a quantity of silk thread; from 20 pounds to 30 pounds was found at Manchester. Wilkinson Greer, of Angel Meadow, Manchester, and another person were committed for trial.

The mill changed hands in 1846, when it was leased to William Walker, who changed the mill back to cotton spinning. The last mill tenant was Alderman Samuel, but the mill burned down under his tenancy in the early 1870s (not an uncommon occurrence in those days).

COWBROOK MILL,

SHEFFIELD ROAD, GLOSSOP.

CATALOGUE

OF THE

MACHINERY

FOR

Preparing and Spinning Cotton,

COMPRISING

17,602 MULE SPINDLES,

By PARR, CURTIS & MADELEY, and PREPARATION MACHINERY for same;
SLUBBING, INTERMEDIATE, and ROVING BOBBINS; PACKING SKIPS, BASKETS,
LEATHER STRAPPING; about

9,760 lbs. AMERICAN COTTON, in process;

600 lbs. YARN, in Cop;

NEW MILL STORES;

CONTENTS of MECHANICS' SHOP: Excellent OFFICE FURNITURE and Effects:

Also, in the event of the Mill not being sold in One Lot, the

LANCASHIRE STEAM BOILER,

30 ft. long by 7 ft. dia.;

HORIZONTAL CONDENSING STEAM ENGINE,

30 in. Cylinder, 4 ft. stroke, by J. C. KAY, Bolton:

80-Horse Power TURBINE,

With GOYT and FITTINGS; and the whole of the

MILL GEARING, SHAFTING, PIPING, &c.,

THEREIN; WHICH WILL BE

SOLD BY AUCTION,

BY

EDWARD RUSHTON, SON & KENYON,

On WEDNESDAY, MAY 11th, 1898,

ON THE PREMISES AS ABOVE.

Sale to commence at 11-30 in the forenoon prompt.

May be Viewed any working day one week prior to Sale.

DESCRIPTIVE CATALOGUES may be had from the AUCTIONEERS, 13, Norfolk Street,
Manchester; and further information from Mr. J. W. TWERDALE, Solicitor, Glossop; or from
Mr. THEO. WALTER ELLISON, Solicitor, Glossop.

Copy of Cowbrook Mill catalogue cover. The small print reads: 'Also in the event of the Mill not being sold in One Lot...', and it then goes on to list the articles excluded from the sale. As Edward Platt bought the mill in 1901, it may be assumed that the materials, and so on, were indeed sold in one lot.

Milltown Mill, Howard Town

'Erected for the spinning of cotton', according to an old document. The mill was leased to Thomas Shaw, cotton manufacturer, of Lower Mill, on 10 February 1803. It was situated in the New Croft area, bounded to the east by the road from Glossop to Whitfield and to the south by Glossop Brook. This mill was owned and managed by the partnership of Thomas Shaw and John Beesley, and was assessed at the time as £38 10s. By 1831, the sole owner was John Beesley, and the assessment had doubled to 375 mill-hands, operating 5,700 spindles. By 1838, the mill changed hands to Messrs Daniel Hodgson and Jonathan Wright. They both lived at Milltown. On 27 January 1842, a fire broke out, and the following account was reported in the *Manchester Guardian* on Wednesday 2 February 1842:

> Cotton Mill Burned Down
> Destructive Fire at Glossop
> Early on Wednesday morning, a destructive fire occurred by Wright and Hodgson, spinners and weavers. The fire was discovered about 2 o'clock in the morning by a person passing at the time, and who immediately gave the alarm, but the inhabitants of the neighbourhood being wrapped in sleep, a long time had elapsed before assistance could be obtained. On the arrival of the engines the devouring element had gained so great ascendance, that they were wholly insufficient to arrest the progress of the flames, and in a short time the entire mill, with its valuable machinery worth £2,000 was totally destroyed. The property we are sorry to hear is only partially insured.

When Milltown Mill burned down, John Wood, together with his brother and their firm, Bros & Co., who already owned Narrow Mill on the same site, moved in smartly and bought the defunct Milltown Mill outright. One of the leases, dated 3 May 1803, related to a reservoir and the Great Eastern Weaving Shed. The Great Eastern Weaving Shed comprised two mills joined together in length, one being narrower than the other (having been built at different times). Within a year of buying Milltown Mill, John Wood had the mill fully operable and making a profit.

Also on the Howard Town site was Old Mill and Burgess' Mill. The latter was demolished in 1859 to make way for the Commercial Mill, which was built in 1860. Old Mill, built for cotton manufacture, contained a steam engine, originally constructed by Peel & Williams at their Soho Foundry, in Manchester. The steam engine was transferred from Old Mill to Shepley's Brookfield Mill where it worked until the mill was gutted by fire some years later.

Bridge End Mill, or Bridge Mill, or Howard Town

Built on land first known as 'Greater Bottoms', the mill stood in the vicinity of where Victoria Bridge (1837) now stands, over the Glossop Brook. It was always kept scrupulously whitewashed, which gave it a distinctive clean appearance. It was built originally as a fulling mill when the first lease was taken out on December 1782 by Robert Fielding, manufacturer, of Whitfield, John Thornley (1747–1790), brother of Robert Thornley from Hadfield, and Samuel Roberts, a clothier from Dinting. On 2 September 1800, George Burgess, woollen manufacturer from Manchester, took a lease for additional land known as 'Greater Bottoms', close to Glossop Brook. In June 1811, Mr Burgess, known to his workpeople as 'Bandy-legged Burgess', was married to a Miss Howe, daughter of the Revd Howe of Glossop Parish Church. Mr Burgess proved to be an unsuccessful cotton manufacturer, and the mill was put up for sale by public auction at the Howard Arms Inn on 5 March 1813. The rental at that time was £150 per annum. The successful bidder was Mr John Wood, who purchased the mill for £1,900. Although the official name of the mill was Bridge End Mill, John Wood referred to it as Howard Town Mills, a name by which it is still known today.

The Weaving Shed – power-loom weaving (from Edward Baines' book, *History of the Cotton Manufacture in Great Britain*, published in 1835).

Opposite above: Howard Town Mills. The Gate House and wing walls at the original entrance to Howard Town Mills in Victoria Street, Glossop, are listed as buildings of historic interest. Note the tower (top left of picture) housing the water supply tank. (Photograph courtesy of *Glossop Chronicle*)

Opposite below: Magnificent Howard Town Mills. (Photograph courtesy of Aerial Photographs Ltd)

J. Wood's Howard Town Mill and Gas Plant. Gas Works in foreground.

At the time that John Wood bought the Howard Town Mills, he was also working three other mills in Glossop, including the Charlestown Mills, first built in 1792. In the early 1800s there was always a scarcity of mill-hands, so he imported many people from the Yorkshire towns. By 1819, under John Wood's extraordinary management, Howard Town Mills expanded, and the number of spindles increased from 5,580 to 38,500; similarly, the number of looms increased from 143 to 916.

In 1822, to encourage qualified mill-workers from far afield to join his workforce, John Wood decided to build accommodation for his mill-hands and staff. For this purpose he purchased three parcels of land:

(a) Land known as High Field, near the premises of colliers Pear Tree Inn.
(b) Houses known as the Step Row.
(c) 16–24 High Street East.

In 1824, Wood purchased further land to the south of Long Mill which he already leased, totalling over 11,000 sq. yards. In 1835 he bought land on Victoria Street, leading to the Norfolk Arms Inn, and he also purchased 2–14a High Street. On this land he built offices and houses. Wood went on to purchase other land including land to the west of Yorkshire Street and High Street, near Lower Bottoms.

Around this time, John Wood bought a family residence – Howard Town House in High Street – which had originally been built by James Owen, another cotton manufacturer. The house was situated near to the gable end of the Old Pear Tree Inn. In 1926, he decided to have gas installed in all his premises, so he purchased more land near Mill Street and the Glossop Brook, for the erection of a gas plant. This large gas works was built by Thomas Bowers & Co.

It was reputed that when the Bishop of Lichfield visited Glossop to dedicate Whitfield Church, he stayed overnight in the Wood family home and, on retiring for the night and being unfamiliar with gaslight, managed to blow out the gas lamp, leaving gas to escape into his bedroom. Sleeping with his window wide open saved him from certain death.

Thomas Shaw was a former owner of Lower Mill and a former leaseholder of Milltown Mill. When he died he was succeeded by his son, Charles Dean, who also inherited ownership of land bordering John Wood's land in the surrounding area. When John Wood bought the mill, water was a precious commodity for all mill-owners, and he had a dispute with Charles Dean over the amount of water he was entitled to have flowing into his mill weir. This led to a lawsuit which was won by John Wood, and resulted in a name plate being fixed in the millyard which read: 'This is to certify that the north-west end of the Bridge End Mill weir, as ascertained by award, is to be 6ft 5½in deep at all times.'

John Wood had a good working relationship with his thirty spinners, who spoke well of him. Many remained in his employment for many years. Their average wage was over £2 per week, and was paid fortnightly. He had no room for shirkers and, as a cotton master, he was fully equal to the task, speaking their kind of language if need be. Unlike some other cotton masters of the district, he would lend them money and supply them with food in times of distress. While they were working, John Wood was reputed to supply buttermilk to those who wanted it, and when men had to work overtime he was know to supply them with a tankard of ale. Candles were supplied to weavers by the company, but normal mill practice was that spinners had to supply their own. In all of Wood's mills he supplied both the weavers and the spinners with free candles. John Wood did not believe in verbal agreements – he insisted that agreements were properly signed and duly witnessed by one of his clerks. The following extracts from the company journal make interesting reading:

July 1st 1825. Purchased from J. Wilson & Sons, Penistone, fifteen pecks of beans, delivered at Saltersbrook on the 10th inst. by 10 o'clock.

November 16th 1825. Received from Joseph Waites, fifty weavers candlesticks.

March 13th 1826. Charles Gartside engaged to point new warehouse windows, inside and outside at 3d per window. These warehouse windows were glazed by Joseph Higginbottom.

April 20th 1826. John Bridge agrees to take a cottage belonging to Mr Wood at Bridge End at the rate of 2s per week, and agrees to quit the cottage in two months from this date without further notice.

April 26th 1826. Memorandum of a return made to the Assessor of Taxes this year, William Thorpe, viz., the clerk; one horse for private use, six draught horses, one dog – paper delivered this day by William Bramald.

October 1st 1826. Robert Byron of Ashton, veteran sergeant physic and doctor to keep in good healthy condition Mr John Wood's eight horses, at the rate of £2 each horse per annum, for the space of twelve months.

December 25th 1826. Copy of notice to give up thirteen cottages near Waterloo Mill, which I now hold and rent from you and from and after that day the respective tenants will then be accountable to you for rent. On the other side you will find a list of the present occupiers of the thirteen cottages. Yours respectfully, John Wood.

December 26th 1826. Reply from the agent Robert Bennett at Barracks Row naming the thirteen tenants and accepting possession of the thirteen cottages and asking for the keys to be delivered to him and requesting to have broken windows repaired. A footnote was added: 'The neighbourhood was not called Roughtown for nothing, many Irish immigrants live in this area.'

Other interesting information from the company journal includes prices in the year 1825:

September 13th. Grinding three pairs of scissors, 4p.

September 17th. Crowther and Hadfield, drink whilst making joints in the pipe of the boiler house, 1s.

October 18th. Drink for men working at engine all night, 5s.

June 12th. John Minshull, cleaning clock in warehouse, 2s.

March 10th 1826. Postage of a letter to London, 1s.

July 12th 1826. James and Samuel Downes, haymaking, one day, 2s 8p and 5s 4p.

December 24th 1826. Expenses at, to and from, Stockport to Macclesfield, 10s.

When John Wood died in 1854, his sons, Samuel, Daniel, and John, took over where their father left off. They were excellent business partners and generous benefactors to the town. Daniel built a family home at Moorfield, and lived there together with his brother Samuel and Samuel's wife, Anne Kershaw, noted for her strong character and unbending energy. With land gifted to the Wood family by Lord Howard, Anne created a 12-acre park with landscape gardens brought up from London. This magnificent park, which cost her £6,000 to create, was named Victoria Park in recognition of the Golden Jubilee of Queen Victoria. The park's name was later changed to Howard's Park. On the same gifted land from Lord Howard, Samuel, together with his brother John, built a cottage hospital, known as Wood's Hospital, and a swimming baths near the entrance of the park. John and Hannah regularly attended Glossop Parish church, and did sterling work in the restoration of the church and the church school. Daniel, by now an alderman of Glossop, retired in 1873. Samuel was also a member of the council for twelve years and, during this period, he was Mayor four times. Both Samuel and Daniel died in the same year, 1888, and Anne had a monument erected in their honour, which stands today at the entrance to the park. In 1912, the family changed their name to Hill Wood in recognition of their grandfather's wife, the Miss Hill from Liverpool. Anne's son, another John, Sir Samuel Hill Wood, was MP for the High Peak from 1910 to 1929. Bridge End Mill, which had become part of the Howard Town Mills, closed down in 1957.

Cross Cliffe Mill

On 24 November 1782, John Newton took out a lease from the Lord of the Manor to build a mill at Cross Cliffe, on the Hurst Brook. Newton was from humble beginnings, and had been a labourer in Whitfield. The date when this mill actually came operational is unclear, but if it was 1783, as is suggested, the mill would have been one of the first purpose-built cotton mills in the area. The mill burned down in 1868, and was then rebuilt some time later, when it became part of Wood's Mill in Howard Town. Demolished in 1902, houses now occupy the Cross Cliffe Mill site, which is named Croft Manor.

Waterloo Mill

Originally Lower Water Mill (Glossop), it was renamed after the great victory of Wellington over Bonaparte. Old Mill and Twist Mill were among the various names given to the mills built on this land, the lease of which dates from 1 August 1807.

When advertised to be sold on 20 April 1809, the mill was described as being three storeys high, plus lofts, 99ft long, and 31ft wide. The mill was powered by a waterwheel, driven via two goits, or sluices, from Shelf Brook. The mill included thirteen houses known as Barrack Row, together with warehouses. In 1815, John Wood & Bros Ltd acquired the lease, and, in 1825, when he sold the mill, it operated 8,666 spindles. The mill was unoccupied from 1831, and remained so for fifteen years. While it was empty a cockfight took place at the mill for £5 aside between Cock Sams, of New Mills, and John Holden's noted cock, Big Willy. Admission cost 3d each, and the fight was talked about for weeks before and after the match (cockfighting is still lawfully practised to this day in the Philippines). John Holden was the toll collector at Dinting Toll Bar. In 1846, Mr Thomas Leigh became the tenant, and then, in September 1851, Mr John Newton Winterbottom took a twenty-one-year lease, at a rental of £300. The mill was burned down on 29 May 1879.

Shepley's Mill, or Wharf Mill

The mill lease, dated from 20 October 1784, was first granted to John Shepley, yeoman, of Glossop, brother to Samuel Shepley. The mill was situated on land south of Shelf Brook. John Shepley also owned the Wesley Street Mill. John's youngest son, Joshua, built the Royal Oak Inn on Sheffield Road to accommodate the stagecoaches and their passengers when the stagecoaches began running from Manchester to Sheffield. The stables of the inn were built alongside the road and a relay of fresh horses was stabled there to facilitate an efficient changeover. The mill ceased to function in 1851.

LITTLE-KNOWN COTTON MILLS OF GLOSSOP AND LONGDENDALE

Observing the cotton mills of Glossop from historic photographs and old Ordnance Survey maps dated 1897 and before, it is amazing there is insufficient intelligence available on many of these formidable-looking mills. Two typical examples of mills lacking information are Gnat Hole Mill and Bent Meadow Mill (see photographs overleaf).

Finally, it must be remembered that cotton mills often changed names and ownership several times during their existence, including mills burned down or demolished, and then rebuilt on the same site as each other, often taking the same name and at other times being renamed.

Some mills were named locally after the owner's Christian name or surname, further confusing the issue, i.e. Shepley's. Mills observed to be functioning within the Glossop area of which there is little or no relevant information are listed as follows: Arundel Street Mill; Barrack Mill on the Shelf Brook (built around 1807, burned down 1879); Bankswood Mill; Boggart Mill; Clark's Mill; Wards Mill; Grain Mill; Hadfield's Lodge Mill; Hole House Mill; Knott's Mill; Tip Woollen Mill; Dinting Mill, which became part of Potter's Print Works; Primrose Mill; Whitfield Mill; Burymewick Mill; Jumble Mill; Simmondley Mill; Coobes Mill; Warth Mill; Rolfes Mill; Braddock's Mill; Barrack Mill; Hawkshead Mill; Holehouse Mill.

Gnat Hole Mill, Glossop.

Bent Mill, Bentmeadow, Hollingworth.

Compstall Mills, Compstall. Back view from Montagu Street, looking south-west. The water visible in the lodges is used for processing. (2/17)

Compstall Mills, Compstall. Front of mill on Andrew Street, and southerly wings adjoining the river Etherow, looking north-east. (2/17)

Chadwick Printworks, Romiley. This picture was taken in 1954, from the east side of Otterspool
Bridge, looking east-north-east. The river Goit, flowing from right to left, lies between the fields in the
foreground and the works. (3/1)

Other cotton mills sourced and powered by the River Etherow were:
Compstall Mills, Compstall, built before 1828, for calico printing, cotton spinning and
manufacture and owned by Edward and James Andrew. It changed ownership in the same year,
with Andrew Bruckshaw & Co. taking over. It was a very large works of over 3 acres. The mill
was built mostly in brick. It had a large, arched, high weir across the river and side lodge to
supply water to the huge waterwheel named 'The Compstall Lily', which was erected in 1838,
and sometimes known as 'The Water Lily'. 'Lily' was reputed to be the largest mill waterwheel
in the world, certainly the largest in the British Isles, and known at that time as 'the wonder
of the age', with thousands visiting her from all parts of the country. She had an immense
overshot wheel, 51ft in diameter and 24ft wide across the breast, with a nominal 350hp. In 1843,
the mill belonged to George Andrew & Sons, employing over 2,000 people, and continued
more or less until 1902 when it became Calico Printers Association Ltd. In 1934, it had new
owners, Graveside & Co. (of Manchester Ltd, branch of CPA Ltd). The final known owners
were Compstall Mills (CPA Ltd) George Andrew & Sons Ltd. It boasted a large, varied selection
of manufacture: rayon, crepe de chine, crepes, fancy figured cloths (rayon), piques (rayon),
poplins, pyjama cloths, rayon fabrics, fancies, shirting, spun rayon, and typewriter cloth. The mill
supported 400 employees in 1944, and in 1953 the mill was still operating, with a workforce of 310
employees.

Chadwick Printworks, Romiley. View from the wooded slope above the south-east bank of the river Goit (at bend) looking north-west. (3/1)

Chadwick Printworks, Romiley

A dyeworks built before 1792. In 1834, the mill was used for calico printing, and the owners were Addison & Siddal. It was an extensive yet fairly old works of nearly 2 acres, with weir, goit and several lodges. Turbine-driven, the mill had its own bore hole with a large treatment plant and elevated storage tanks, water being extensively used for processing. The mill changed hands in 1850 to Joseph Lawson Siddall. After forty years it changed names again to Sydall Bros (branch of, and agents for, CPA Ltd). The type of manufacture changed from calico printing to dyers and finishers when the mill was taken over in 1934 by the Calico Printers Association Ltd, who produced silk and rayon goods. By 1953, the works employed 190 people.

Along the banks of the river Etherow in the Compstall area, there were four known cotton manufacturing mills, and, in Romiley, at least two mills. The larger town of Stockport possessed many mills with at least five large known cotton spinning and weaving mills.

NEW HOMES FOR OLD COTTON MILLS

Many of the cotton mills throughout the North of England have, over the years, been completely demolished, and many smaller sites are now occupied by housing.

In Glossop, Wren Nest Mills, of the 1820s industrial age, is one such large mill that has been awakened by an injection of £15 million, breathing new life into the five-storey cotton mill of old. She has been tastefully converted into four floors of seventy-two two-bedroom apartments, embracing allocated car parking space and high-quality shops. A restaurant is expected to be added to form a pleasing environment in this long-awaited development.

Howard Town Mills was known simply as 'Wood's' to the hundreds of mill-hands who once worked there. In 2004, she also received the necessary planning permission to go ahead and transform the site into a tasteful thirty-six homes, with a retail complex (to include high-quality shops and stores, a restaurant, and a pub), and to transform one mill building into fifty-six homes. The proposals also included public car parking and a walkway through a colonnade for the benefit of pedestrians. Howard Town Mills lies in the town centre within 1 mile of Wren Nest Mills. Both mills have once more become an asset, adding prestige, and benefiting the people of Glossopdale. Queen Cotton would be proud.

XV

THE COTTON INDUSTRY IN DECLINE –
THE HOWARD FAMILY LEAVE
IT ALL BEHIND

The Howard family will never be forgotten in Glossop – there are far too many reminders in the town for that to happen. The Dukes and the Barons of Glossop were the wealthiest of all the mill-owners, both in the Glossopdale and Longdendale area. The influence of the Howards commenced in the 1700s and certainly continued right through until they departed in 1925.

They owned many large mills along Padfield Brook and the river Etherow, bringing added wealth and success to the district. They built the Town Hall in 1837, followed by a new Market Hall in 1844. In addition they built Glossop a new grammar school in 1851 – the Duke of Norfolk's (later to become the Infant Dept of the Duke of Norfolk C of E School) – adjoining the Parish Church. Mathew Ellison's son, Mathew Ellison Hadfield, became chief architect to the Duke of Norfolk, and he and his son and grandson designed the magnificent Victoria Hall and many other distinctive buildings.

Other important gifts donated to the town from the Duke's family included the land for Victoria Hall, Partington Home, Wood's Hospital, the Baths, and Manor Park. A chateau-style former entrance lodge to the Howard estate, from the Old Glossop side, still stands today within the park's boundary.

Lord Howard was angered by the Manchester, Sheffield and Lincolnshire Railway Company, who refused his request to add a branch line to their existing railway in order to serve the townsfolk of Glossopdale and Manchester. It was a very sensible and feasible suggestion and the indefatigable Lord was not to be beaten. He knew only too well that he and all the mill-owners and businessmen in the area would benefit. They decided to go ahead and be accountable themselves for the construction of the branch line and district railway stations. Work on the branch line began in November 1842, and was completed and officially opened on 25 June 1845. The railway station, which is within Glossop's town centre, was built in 1847, with a friendly life-size stone lion, copied from Duke's own coat of arms and standing proudly over the station entrance, a silent witness to his master. It is conveniently close to the Norfolk Arms where people still occasionally swap yarns on the grand cotton mills and print works of old. The many railway commuters between Glossop and Manchester should be forever thankful for the Duke's vision of a railway line to Manchester and beyond.

The Duke of Norfolk's family, being of proud Catholic faith, showed their support to Glossop Catholicism when the 1st Baron Howard of Glossop built the imposing Church of St Charles Borromeo, Hadfield. It was officially opened on 18 February 1858 by Lord Howard, together with his wife, Lady Augusta, the 1st Baroness. In 1885, the 2nd Baron of Glossop demolished the Lady Chapel to make way for a family vault, which was completed in 1888, and where he reburied his parents and his younger brother Charles, who had died in 1861. Both the 2nd and and 3rd Barons and their wives were buried at St Charles, Hadfield, thus completing the line of Barons of Glossop buried there. On the death of the 3rd Baron in 1972, the title was referred back to his son, Miles Francis Stapleton Fitzalan-Howard, 17th Duke of Norfolk (see Appendix I, page 155).

Parting is always tinged with sadness, and so it was for the parting of the ways of the Howard family, coinciding, many will say, with the decline of the cotton industry in the 1920s. After over 300 years of influence in the Dales of Derbyshire, evidenced by the many places named after them, the 3rd Lord Howard of Glossop and his wife, Lady Beaumont, 11th Baroness Beaumont, a peer in her own right, decided to call it a day, sell off their Glossop estates and mills, and move to Carlton Towers, Lady Beaumont's family seat in Yorkshire.

It was a very disturbing and sad day when letters dropped through the letter boxes of all the Glossopdale tenants informing them that the Lord of the Manor had decided to quit his residence and move to Yorkshire. It was even more disturbing when the tenants each received a communication:

Notices to Quit – All yearly Lady-Day tenants of the agricultural and small holdings and gardens were duly served with notices to quit expiring Lady Day, 1926.

Stepping back in time, one cannot help thinking that it was Mathew Ellison, the Duke's agent, who had inspired the Duke to build Glossop Hall. He wrote with loyalty and conviction to his employer, saying:

The Glossop estate differs from any other portion of Your Grace's family property, in that from a state of comparative obscurity and inconsiderable rental, it has during the last forty years attained an exalted and influential position.

No doubt fired by this philanthropic praise and encouragement from his astute agent, in 1851, Lord Howard built his prestigious new luxury home, Glossop Hall – 'a finely proportioned structure erected in the French Chateau style of stone with slate and leaded roofs and Belvedere over the south wing'. The description continues: 'The Hall was approached through a pair of massive iron gates, with rusticated stone piers surmounted by stone ball ornaments, leading up a winding carriage drive, through an avenue of lime and sycamore trees, terminating in a wide terraced gravel walk running the length of the Residence.' And like every residence fit for a Lord, it had its own 'beamed and panelled ceiling and grained marble mantelpiece, overlooking the ornamental conservatory'.

In the general notes of the auction catalogue, it reads:

The properties are situated in and around the important cotton manufacturing town of Glossop and the villages of Dinting, Hadfield, Padfield, Charlesworth, Simmondly, Marple Bridge, Chisworth, and Chunal.

The railway stations of Glossop, Hadfield, Dinting Junction, and Marble Bridge bring practically the whole estate within easy access of the adjoining vast industrial district, with Manchester, the

NORTH DERBYSHIRE

In and around the Town of GLOSSOP, 13 miles from MANCHESTER and 18 miles from SHEFFIELD

Particulars, Plans & Conditions of Sale

— OF —

The Important Freehold

Residential, Agricultural and Sporting Estate

GLOSSOP DALE

extending to an area of about

7,400 Acres

and situate in the Townships of

**GLOSSOP, LUDWORTH, CHISWORTH, MELLOR,
CHARLESWORTH, SIMMONDLEY, DINTING, PADFIELD,
HADFIELD, WHITFIELD and CHUNAL.**

To be offered for Sale by Auction by

Messrs. **KNIGHT, FRANK & RUTLEY**

(Sir Howard Frank, Bt., G.B.E., K.C.B., John Frederick Knight, F.A.I., Alfred John Barrows, F.S.I., and Arthur Horace Knight, F.A.I.)

ACTING IN CONJUNCTION WITH

Messrs. **COLLINS & COLLINS**

(H. J. Collins, F.A.I., and A. P. Saunders, F.S.I.)

AND

Messrs. **WILLIAM DAVIES & SON**

(William Davies, F.A.I., Frank A. Davies, F.A.I., and Wm. D. Lawson, A.A.I.)

*At the Victoria Hall, Glossop, on Wednesday and Thursday, the
16th and 17th days of September, 1925, at 11.0 and 2.30 o'clock
on the former day, and 11.0 o'clock on the latter day
(unless previously sold privately).*

Solicitors: Messrs. STAMFORD & READ, The Hall, Glossop, and 48, Market Street, Bradford; Messrs. BAND, HATTON & CO., 9 and 11, High Street, Coventry.

Auctioneers: Messrs. COLLINS & COLLINS, 37, South Audley Street, London, W. 1; Messrs. WILLIAM DAVIES & SON, 9, Albert Square, Manchester; and Messrs. KNIGHT, FRANK & RUTLEY, 20, Hanover Square, London, W. 1; and at Edinburgh, Glasgow and Ashford (Kent).

Copies of the Particulars and Conditions of Sale, with Plans, can be obtained of the Auctioneers, or at Glossop Hall, at the price of 2s. 6d. per copy.

Front cover of Glossop Dale catalogue. The most celebrated auction ever to be held in Glossopdale and Longdendale was about to begin.

metropolis of Lancashire, only 11 miles distant from Marple Bridge (a favourite residential area for Mancunians), and 13 miles from Glossop.

Glossop Hall mansion and gardens stood in 70 acres of farmland, and the general notes begin with a description of Glossop Hall as a substantial constructed and comfortable mansion, with grounds and gardens of exceedingly charming character. The Hall led into a ballroom, which was superbly decorated and included fourteen principal and guest bedrooms. For the household staff there were twelve servants' bedrooms, three nurseries, a school room, eight maids' bedrooms, five bathrooms on the top floor, and so the list goes on. The grounds included an Italian garden, terraced lawns, a chain of fishponds, woods and parklands. The fourteen horse stables included men's living accommodation and, of course, three coach houses and two lodge entrances and small holdings.

Lord Howard of Glossop once owned more than 7,400 acres of land in Glossop and the surrounding villages. The auction included twenty-seven farms, and land ranging from the 2-acre Lower Dinting farm house and cottage to the larger-sized 122-acre Far Bradshaw Farm. There were numerous cottages and residential houses. Also included was the prestigious Easton House, which for many years was home to the late Lord Doverdale. There was a corn mill on the northern side of High Street East, Glossop, and 'a desirable dwelling house, "The Wharf"', near The Cross, Old Glossop. Also included were Blackshaw Quarries and the Sand Pit. Even the historic Roman Melandra Castle went up for sale, surrounded by the 89-acre Lower Gamesley Farm. There was building land, noted grouse moors, allotments, sports fields, even a small reservoir near Dinting Railway Station, and much more.

The first day's sale was on Wednesday 16 September 1925, commencing at 11 a.m. Auctioning Lots 1–101 were included. The second session commenced at 2.30 p.m., with Lots 101–203. The sale was completed on the second day with one session only, commencing at 11 a.m. There is little information regarding the two day sales, but some interesting recorded prices paid for properties are as follows:

LOT	DESCRIPTION	COST
122	Impressive Gamesly Farm - including the historic Roman Melandra Castle	£1,300
228	Magnificent Glossop Hall - mansion and gardens	£8,500
	Glossop Hall's surrounding land	£7,000
	Coachman's Bungalow Lodge	£850
230	Imposing Easton House - for many years former residence of Lord Doverdale	£1,200
231	The Corn Mill - consisting of 4 floors with sack room and offices	£750
232	The Wharf - desirable dwelling house near The Cross, Old Glossop	£450

The number of lots actually sold during the two day sale was seemingly disappointing, but this benefitted many tenants by allowing them to enjoy their tenancy for many years.

As the sale ended, so too the Howard era ended, leaving behind it worry and unhappiness and a bleak uncertain future of short-time working for many of the Howards' former employees and their families. Yet, despite this, in the obituary of the 1st Baron he was credited with being 'the pioneer and champion of deliverance during the Cotton Famine', which he surely was.

The once famous Glossop Hall was replaced by the Kingsmoor School, but this too has disappeared, and where once beautiful architecture and spacious, well laid-out glorious gardens appeared, homes for new generations now stand. Some things are everlasting: the Duke of Norfolk and the Barons of Glossop will forever be in the heart of the community. The Dukes of Norfolk and the subsequent Lord Howards were once the very heartbeat of the town of Glossop.

XVI

GLOSSOP'S NATIONAL COTTON QUEEN OF GREAT BRITAIN

As the demand for British Cotton began its slow decline and mill-owners began laying their workers on short-time, Cotton Queens were an early attempt to advertise and raise the profile of cotton both at home and abroad and to promote and encourage people to wear more attractive cool cotton merchandise.

The intention was also to raise the morale of the cotton workers within the industry. Only mill-girls could compete, so it offered them an exclusive glamourous role – reigning as Cotton Queen for one year and working away from home and their drab mill. There would be an enchanting crowning ceremony for them to look forward to. It would be an alluring occasion tinged with romantic associations, to help stifle the humdrum existence the girls endured, working in the hot, noisy, smelly atmosphere of mill shed life.

The event was sponsored by the cotton industry, with the *Daily Dispatch*, a leading newspaper of the day, chosen to organise and promote the event and to search the land for the first National Cotton Queen of Great Britain, who would reign for twelve unforgettable months. The girl chosen had to be employed within the cotton industry and be between sixteen and twenty-five years of age. She would not just be a pretty face, for she would be expected to converse effortlessly and to write and deliver all her own speeches, and be capable of playing an ambassadorial role on behalf of the entire cotton industry. The successful Cotton Queen would have to agree to undergo three months' training in elocution, deportation, and etiquette, to provide her with the confidence and poise required for this fascinating once-in-a-lifetime role. She would travel the country in a chauffeur-driven car, accompanied by a chaperone, with no more boring mill work for one whole year – it was an exciting prospect for any young mill girl.

The organisers decided to choose six contestants from twelve defined areas in the cotton mill country of the North of England.

Once the competition was announced, the organisers were besieged with applications and photographs from aspiring young mill-girls throughout Derbyshire, Lancashire, and the surrounding areas. Tremendous interest was shown throughout the cotton industry and beyond.

In the Glossop area twelve candidates were selected and they were judged in Glossop's (now demolished) Empire Cinema, where six mill-girls were selected to enter the next round, with their photographs displayed in many of the town's shops and hotels. Glossop's eventual area finalist

Cover of *Daily Dispatch* souvenir programme. (Courtesy of the *Daily Dispatch* newspaper)

Frances Lockett, 1st National Cotton Queen of Great Britain. (Courtesy of the *Glossop Chronicle*)

was nineteen-year-old Miss Frances Lockett who worked in a mill in Hyde. Crowds lined the streets as her procession paraded through the town for her eventual Glossop Cotton Queen crowning ceremony – only a taste of what was to follow during her exciting days at Blackpool.

Frances joined nineteen other excited finalists from other cotton towns, who went forward on that memorable day to be judged at the Tower Ballroom, Blackpool. The lucky ones were feted in the national newspapers and given maximum publicity. They were dined amidst the flashing cameras of the media and then paraded along Blackpool's famous Golden Mile. Newspapers even hired rickshaws to ferry the district finalists around prior to Saturday's distinguished final at the Tower Circus. The programme of events included being entertained by a grand orchestra and a Cotton Fashion Parade by the House of Reville. This was to be followed by the Grand Parade of the twenty mill girl finalists before the judges retired to make their choice.

The first National Cotton Queen of Great Britain for 1930–31, was triumphantly announced as Miss Glossop – Frances Lockett. Frances wore a red velvet cloak trimmed with ermine for her glamourous coronation, as she was presented with a golden crown.

The Mayor of Blackpool greeted the new Queen amid loud applause and cheers on this prestigious occasion as he made a presentation to her on behalf of the Blackpool Corporation. As winner, the Cotton Queen would also be feted by fashion houses and provided with a substantial wardrobe by famous names which included Marshall & Snelgrove, Debenhams, Liberty, and Affleck & Brown.

Frances remembered the highlights of her reign: 'I did mannequin parades, and attended Cotton Balls and Cotton Weeks at Lewis's and Kendal's and I went all over Great Britain.' With pride she recalled her visit to the Houses of Parliament:

> I had lunch with six cabinet ministers. Mr Ramsey was the Prime Minister and I had an interview with him. He said he wished he was coming to the ball that night at Covent Garden. Then I met Lloyd George [leader of the Liberal Party, Prime Minister 1916–22]. He had a feel of my dress and asked, 'Is this cotton?' I said, 'Oh, yes' and he said, 'It's lovely, I must get Megan [his daughter] to buy some'.

Frances's sad memory was of the 1930s depression which the cotton industry was suffering. She recalled: 'I went to Kendal's Cotton Week, we had them all over the country you see, and I used to go for a week at different places and talk about towels; unfortunately we didn't sell any cotton materials.' There was a tinge of sadness in her voice.

The ninth and last Cotton Queen, Miss Preston, was on official duties in the holiday coastal town of Scarborough when her reign virtually ended as the Second World War was declared in September 1939. This sadly signalled the end of National Cotton Queens of Great Britain.

When the war ended in 1945, the competition was never revived. This was probably due to the demise of the cotton industry, which could no longer support the cost of sponsoring a National Cotton Queen Competition. And ten years later…

Unfortunately, after all its tireless efforts advocating the British cotton industry, the loyal *Daily Dispatch* ceased publication in 1955. For ten years it had guided, helped, and supported all of the following nine Cotton Queens of the North:

Miss Glossop	1930–31
Miss Leigh	1931–32
Miss Burnley	1932–33
Miss Salford	1933–34
Miss Manchester	1934–35
Miss Manchester	1935–36
Miss Bolton	1936–37
Miss Rochdale	1937–38
Miss Stockport	1938–39
Miss Preston	1939–40

Most noticeably, with new skills acquired during their reign, and with a fresh outlook on life, none of the respected, high-profile National Cotton Queens of Great Britain ever returned to their former employment working in hot, noisy, smelly cotton mills.

XVII

DEATH KNELL AND BRASS BELLS –
END OF THE GLORY DAYS
OF THE COTTON INDUSTRY

In the early hours of the morning, from the 1800s to the 1940s, hundreds of mill-girls and boys would walk up Victoria Street and Charlestown, Glossop, New Road and the Bottoms Coach Road, Longdendale, and many other cobbled streets of God's Country in the North. They trudged and shuffled their way to the mill where they worked. Any non-mill-hands who were so fortunate as to be lazing in their warm beds would be wakened to the sounds of the 'Cotton-Mill Symphony', composed of clanging brass mill bells, the clatter of clogs, the rattle of tin enamelled brew cans and cups clashing against the mill-hands' brass belted buckles, and the chattering chorus and laughter echoing throughout the high streets from both the young and the not-so-young cotton workers. Many would stop on their way t' mill and pop int'o shop or bakery to buy cigarettes and matches, or sandwiches and cakes, before continuing to gossip gaily to each other, perhaps about their previous night out or the adventure of their courting and fumbling in the dark behind t' mill. Many were superstitious and, to protect them against financial difficulties, young couples on their wedding night would be expected to sleep on a cotton mattress – otherwise the superstitious folk would not be too pleased with them.

For many, the large brass bells of the cotton mills that rang out in the frosty early morning air to summon the cotton hands to their work before the cocks had time to crow, would peal no more. A nightmare – to some – was about to end: on those cold dark days of winter, the thirty minutes of clanking bells would no longer rouse them from their clinging sultry beds to slip begrudgingly, clog-clad, dragging themselves towards the incandescent gas lights which conveniently fanned down to supply light over the cinder-path shortcuts leading them to their stuffy, foul-smelling, overheated mills. Then the sad fact dawned.

Those irritating, nauseating, clanging brass bells
would no longer call them, 't' work, in't mill'. No
longer could they cling to their comforting weekly
pay packet and their meagre but secure future.

From the 1880s, Glossop's cotton production, like many other North of England cotton towns, was in decline. By the 1900s, the cotton industry was in a downwards spiral, yet 70 per cent of the population still relied on the cotton trade – the bubble that was about to burst!

This was further accentuated during the commercial slump of the First World War. Before 1914, India imported 3,000 million yards of cotton from England. By 1937, this was reduced to 334 million yards. Great Britain suffered a further blow in 1933, when Japan became the world's largest cotton manufacturer after she introduced twenty-four-hour cotton production.

Shocked by the 1930s trade slump throughout the land, Glossop and Longdendale once more had one of the worst unemployment rates in Britain. The death knell had truly sounded. Wakes Week at Blackpool seemed a dream away. Happily for Glossop, other employment was provided by Messrs Olive and Partington's larger paper mills, the Dinting Vale Print Works, and Calico Printers.

Between the wars, 345,000 mill-workers left the cotton industry and 800 mills closed. By the 1950s, Longdendale and Glossopdale, together with over 3,000 other mills in Northern England, no longer relied on manufacturing cotton goods for their livelihood.

When war was declared in 1939, mill-workers became less reliant on their once domineering cotton masters of old. Apart from producing military uniforms, bed sheets, parachutes, and other military necessities for the war effort, both the UK and Japan were no longer producing cloth for the international trade, and the United States forthwith became the major supplier of textiles throughout the world.

The days of the cotton worker had become bleak. And behind the footlights of many of the music halls throughout the North, in pubs and working men's clubs, in the Norfolk Arms of Glossop, and the Bull Inn of Tintwistle, redundant cotton workers would gather around the piano player, to accompany the Saturday night revellers intent upon forgetting their troubles and worries, and perhaps singing lustily the chorus of the song:

It's the rich that gets the credit,
It's the poor that gets the blame,
It's the same the whole world over,
Isn't a bloomin' shame?

Majestic Queen Cotton had reigned nobly and well. It was time for her to move on and flourish elsewhere. For as long as peoples of the world enjoy sleeping between cool cotton sheets and wear crisp cotton shirts, blouses and smart soft cotton frocks, and enjoy the feel of cotton, she will never die. To Northerners she has simply become a well beloved, never to be forgotten, Queen Cotton of the North.

GLOSSARY
COTTON MILL CHATTER

Bobbin — A spool or reel that holds cotton thread or yarn before being taken to a spinning machine.

Cards — Used for untangling the raw cotton.

Carder or Card Stripper — A person who operates a Carding Machine to prepare the cotton for weaving by removing the tangles and knots in the raw cotton and straightening out the fibres.

Card-Nailer or Card Grinder — A person who maintains the teeth on the Carding Machine and repairs cotton fibre Carding Machines.

Cotton Feeder — The person who fed the cotton into the loom.

Cotton Master — The mill-owner or manager who employed people to work in their mills.

Creelers — Their job was to 'fill the creels' (a frame for holding bobbins) to supply the rollers with bobbins.

Doffer — A cylinder which stripped off the raw cotton from the Carding Engine.

Doff the Cops — The person who removed the full bobbin on completion of the spun thread.

Fustian — Any of several thick-twilled cotton fabrics.

Horse Gin — A horse walking in circles harnessed to a crank geared to a shaft and belts to supply power to a small mill.

Jenny — A machine on which a number of threads could be spun at the same time.

Mule	A machine for spinning several threads at once, using water power.
Nap or Short Nap	Fabric with a short fuzzy surface.
Piecers	Their task was to 'piece the yarn', i.e. repair promptly the breaks in the thread.
Putter-out	Worked for a cotton merchant and was responsible for putting out materials and receiving finished cloth from cottage factory weavers.
Rollers	A method by which the thread, as it was spun, was both drawn and twisted at the same time.
Slubber	A person who operates a Slubbing Frame.
Weavers	A person who weaves or interlaces threads to form cloth.
Warp	Threads running from end to end on a piece of cloth.
Weft	Threads running across a piece of cloth.
Winders–Warpers	Workers responsible for preparing the finished yarn for weaving, by aligning the longitudinal threads forming the 'warp' with the cross threads making up the 'weft'.
Winders	A person responsible for winding the thread onto the bobbins. Also a worker looking for flaws while rolling up the finished cloth.
Worsted	A woollen cloth with a smooth face.

APPENDIX I

The Dukes of Norfolk & Baron Howard's of Glossop.

In 1869 the title Baron Howard of Glossop was created for a younger son of the 13th Duke of Norfolk; the eldest son would have inherited his father's title as 14th Duke of Norfolk.

Baron Howard's of Glossop:

Edward George Fitzalan-Howard, 1st Baron Howard of Glossop (1818-1883).

Francis Edward Fitzalan-Howard, 2nd Baron Howard of Glossop (1859-1924)

Bernard Edward Fitzalan-Howard, 3rd Baron Howard of Glossop (1885-1972)

On the death of the 3rd Baron Howard of Glossop in 1972, his title was assigned to his son, Miles Francis Stapleton Fitzalan-Howard, who had already inherited the Barony of Beaumont in 1971, from his mother, Mona Stapleton, the 11th Baroness Beaumont. (please refer to p.144)

As the 16th Duke of Norfolk had four daughters but no sons, on his death in 1975, Miles Francis Stapleton Fitzalan-Howard, 4th Baron Howard of Glossop, and second cousin to the 16th Duke, inherited the title, 17th Duke of Norfolk.

Dukedom of Norfolk – premier peer of the realm and hereditary Earl Marshal of England.

Dukes of Norfolk earliest recorded connections with Glossop (please refer to page 60) through to the present day:

Bernard Edward Howard, 12th Duke of Norfolk (1765-1842).

Henry Charles Howard, 13th Duke of Norfolk (1791-1856).

Henry Granville Fitzalan-Howard, 14th Duke of Norfolk (1815-1860).

Henry Fitzalan-Howard, 15th Duke of Norfolk (1847-1917).

Bernard Marmaduke Fitzalan-Howard, 16th Duke of Norfolk (1908-1975).

Miles Francis Stapleton Fitzalan-Howard, 17th Duke of Norfolk (1915-2002).

Edward William Fitzalan-Howard, 18th Duke of Norfolk (born 1956).

Heir apparent: Henry Miles Fitzalan-Howard, Earl of Arundel and Surrey (born 1987).

Seat or residence of the Dukedom of Norfolk: Arundel Castle.

APPENDIX II

Extracts from Mr Charles Wilson's nine diaries from 1853-1861.

Monday June 26th 1854
Drive to Hadfield, 7-35 train to Manchester. Return by 9-25 train with Chairman and Deputy Chairman to Mottram Station. Visit Marslands (mill owner), Auxiliary Reservoir, Arnfield, Rhodes Wood, Torside and Woodhead.

Saturday 17th November 1855
At Mr Samuel Rhodes, Mottram, at night, in connection with purchase of mills.

Wednesday 3rd February 1856
Obtaining information from Mr Thomas Rhodes in the evening, respecting the capabilities of Bottoms Lodge and Rhodes Mills, for the Chairman of the Water Works Committee.

Tuesday 6th February 1856
With Mr Drinkwater (Dukinfield Water Works Company) examining Turbine at Platts Mill, Hadfield. (Expenses – Gratuity to Engineer at Platts Mill…1/-.)

Monday 25th February 1856
Afterwards drive to Mottram to see Mr Samuel Rhodes respecting purchase of Rhodes Mill.

Tuesday 26th February 1856
Meet Mr Ald. Pilling and Mr Austin at Hadfield Station at 10 a.m. Examining premises at Rhodes's Mill with them.

Saturday 5th April 1856
9-15 train from Hadfield to Manchester. Return by 1-45 train to Hadfield with Ald. Pilling and accompany him and Mr Saml. Rhodes to Bottoms Lodge Mill. Arranging about repairs at the said mill.

Saturday 12th April 1856
At Torside … Afterwards with Mr Taylor and Mr Samul. Rhodes at Bottoms Lodge Mill respecting repairs to flooring etc.

Friday 16th May 1856
Meet Mr Ald. Pilling at Hadfield at 10 a.m. With Mr Pilling all day at Bottoms Lodge Mill, Rhodes's Mill, and Reservoirs in Longdendale. (Expenses – Mr Pilling's Rail Fare Manchester to Hadfield and back, 4/8d)

Saturday 21st June 1856
9-15 train from Hadfield to Manchester. Return by 1-15 train from Hadfield accompanied by Mr Alderman Pilling. Proceed from Hadfield to Bottoms Mill and Rhodes's Mill, thence home. (Expense – Cab from Mr Alderman Pilling's to Railway Station 9d. Expenses – Mr Ald. Pillings Railway Fare, Manchester to Hadfield 2/4d)

Wednesday 3rd September 1856
9-15 train from Hadfield to Manchester. Return by 1-45 train with Sir E. Armitage, Mr Ald. Pilling, and Mr Berry. They return to Manchester by 7-4 train after having been at Torside, Rhodes Wood, Rhodes Mill, and Bottoms Lodge Mill. (Expenses

– cab and Railway fares for Sir E. Armitage, Mr Ald. Pilling, Mr Berry, 15/-.)

Saturday 1st November 1956
Drive to Broadbottom with Mr Thomas Rhodes of Hollingworth. Examine Shuttles and weir belonging to Sidebottoms Mill, Broadbottom. 10-5 train from Broadbottom to Manchester.

Tuesday 23rd December 1856
In Expenses. Revd. J.A. Page, Tintwistle, for Fees for examining Map of Tintwistle in connection with purchase of Bottoms Mill etc. …5/-.

Saturday 14th March 1857
Drove to Torside, thence to Rhodes Mill. Inspecting Rhodes Mill and Bottoms Lodge Mill with Mr Taylor, and Messrs Rhodes and Armstrong.

Friday 20th November 1857
At Crowden Brook with Mr Taylor in the morning turning on water through new line of pipes for Messrs. Brown's Bleachworks. Mr Brown Junr was informed that they must keep the watercourse for taking water out of Crowden Brook open, as the Mill Watercourse might occasionally have to be emptied for repairs. He said they would keep it open.

Monday 14th December 1857
At Torside etc. in the afternoon, and at Auxiliary Reservoir, Milburn's Foundery etc. in the afternoon. Left plan of land at Broadbottom belonging to Mr Bostock at Mr Thomas Rhodes house Hollingworth this afternoon – delivered the plan to Mrs Thomas Rhodes who promised to give it to her husband.

Monday 19th April 1858
At Woodhead with Mr Taylor in the forenoon arranging with him as to the position of a new shaft being sunk (as Requested by Mr Bateman) between the line of proposed new embankment and the Paper Mill.

Monday 17th May 1858
Meet Mr Fisher on behalf of Assignees of Messrs. Rhodes and Armstrong's Estate at Bottoms Lodge for the purpose of taking possession (on behalf of Manchester Corporation) at Bottoms Lodge and Rhodes's Mills, but as the keys have been left at Manchester by the Assignees we cannot get in. I had Mr Saml. Taylor and Mr Saml. Rhodes with me.

Tuesday 18th May 1858
Return by 1-45 train from Manchester to Hadfield with Mr Berry, Mr Saml. Rhodes and Mr Fisher. Examine the whole of the premises at Bottoms Lodge and Rhodes's Mills, and receive the keys from Mr Fisher upon him paying £130 to Mr Berry for back rent and articles belonging to the Corporation which have been sold to the Assignees. – I send the keys to Mr Taylor (by Leeming) with a message for him to put both watchmen on at both mills.

Monday 19th July 1858
At Auxiliary Reservoir and Broadbottom with Mr Austin and Mr Lynde obtaining evidence respecting flow of water at Marsland's Mill, Best Mill. Afterwards drove over to Stalybridge with Mr Austinto [to] see Nicholas Booth, who formerly worked at Marsland's Mill.

Saturday 31st July 1858
Drive to Denton – meet Ald. Sir E. Armitage & Ald. Pilling, return with them and go with them to Mr Marsland's at Best Mill. I wait at Broadbottom while they have interview with Messrs Marsland's (owners Best Hill Mills, Broadbottom). Afterwards return with them to Mottram.

Thursday 22nd December 1859
With Mr Austin and Mr Richard Austin at Tintwistle obtaining evidence, Hull V Corporation of Manchester.

Monday 23rd January 1860
At Auxiliary Reservoir and at Bankwood Mill (Waller V Corporation) afterwards at Manchester. (Wailer was mill owner of Bankwood Works.)

Saturday 18th February 1860
At Manchester per Railway from Hadfield to
Manchester and back. Afterwards at Auxiliary
Reservoir getting information from Mr Stafford
etc. respecting Bankwood Mill – Wailer V
Corporation.

Saturday 31st March 1860
At Tintwistle all day etc. in Wailer and Another V
Corporation. Mr Austin at Tintwistle part of the day.

Monday 2nd April 1860
Bower at Chisworth with Mr – in Walter V
Corporation.

Tuesday 3rd April 1860
At Manchester per Railway from Hadfield with
return ticket but did not return by Railway
having to go with Mr Hawksley from Manchester
to Rhodes Wood Mill etc. in a carriage. (Mr
Hawksley was M.C.W.W. Consulting Engineer.)

Wednesday 4th April 1860
At Liverpool on trial Waller and Another V
Corporation per Railway from Tintwistle to
Liverpool.

Thursday 5th April 1860
At Liverpool and Manchester per Railway from
Liverpool to Manchester, and from thence to
Tintwistle.

Saturday 9th June 1860
At the reservoirs all day – making experiments at
Gauge Basin, Rhodes Wood in connection with
the discharging 55 cu.ft. per minute.

Monday 24th September 1860
At Torside etc. At Manchester & back per Railway.
At Bottoms Lodge Mill inspecting opening
windows at end of Mill opposite blowing room
and putting additional skylights in Mill.

Friday 26th April 1861. At Rhodes Mill, then
Hadfield to Manchester per railway.

Monday 24th December 1860
Hadfield to Glossop per Railway – At Estate
Office there respecting Conveyance of Land
– Auxiliary Reservoir.

Auxiliary Reservoir: Constructed c. 1850, of
approx. four and a half million gallons capacity
with River diversion and sluices. Situated 2.08
miles downstream of Bottoms Gauge Basin, at
Melandra – due west of the Merlandra Castle.

Monday 23rd December 1861
Meet Mr Austin and Mr Holker at Messrs.
Shepley's, Brookfield. In the works, and from
thence to Woodhead with them all day with
reference to Wailer V Corporation.

INDEX